PRACTISE YOUR
CALCULATOR
SKILLS

Nigel Langdon

Edited by Helen Davies
Designed by Graham Round

**Illustrated by Naomi Reed, Martin Newton, Rob McCaig,
Mark Longworth and Graham Round**

Contents

About this book

This is a book of puzzles and number games to help you practise your calculator skills. It starts with simple puzzles and tricks which will improve your speed and accuracy on a calculator. Then you can move on to more advanced problems, involving powers, roots, statistics and trigonometry, and there are puzzles to do on a scientific calculator. Throughout the book you will find simple explanations of the mathematics you need to do the calculations. All the answers are given at the back on pages 42 to 47.

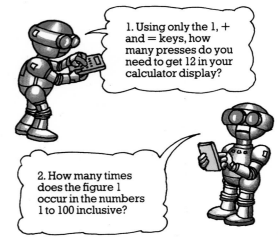

1. Using only the 1, + and = keys, how many presses do you need to get 12 in your calculator display?

2. How many times does the figure 1 occur in the numbers 1 to 100 inclusive?

Types of calculators

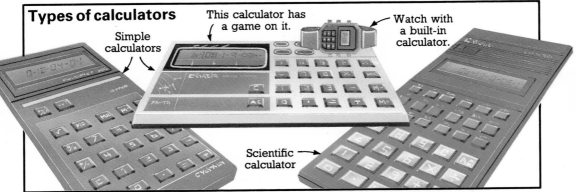

Simple calculators

This calculator has a game on it.

Watch with a built-in calculator.

Scientific calculator

Most people have simple calculators with keys for everyday calculations, such as adding numbers and finding percentages. Scientific calculators have lots of extra keys, but most of these just provide short cuts, doing jobs which you could do yourself on a simple calculator, such as calculating powers or entering sums with brackets.

The operations a calculator can do (adding, subtracting and so on) are sometimes called functions. The symbols for the functions vary from one calculator to another. If the symbols on yours are different from those in this book, check them in the instruction manual that came with the calculator.

On scientific calculators, opposite or "inverse" functions, such as squaring and finding square roots, are put on the same key. To select the second function you press a key marked INV (short for inverse). The labels for functions are often colour coded so you can tell which is selected by the INV key.

3

Keyboard puzzles

The puzzles on these two pages will help you get familiar with the positions of the basic keys on a calculator.

When you enter a calculation make sure you press the keys firmly and quickly. If your finger hovers too long over a key you may enter a number twice. If you do enter a wrong number you can correct it by pressing the Clear Entry key. This wipes out only the number you have just entered so you do not have to start the whole sum again. Before starting a new calculation always press the All Clear key to erase the whole of the last sum from the calculator.

2. See if you can make the calculator display 100 by pressing only these keys.

Can you do it with only ten presses?

3. Try to make 1001 appear in the display using only these keys.

2 7 × − =

How many presses did it take you? A good score is less than ten.

4. Six whole numbers will divide exactly into 1001. Can you work out what they are?

5. Can you work out which operation keys (+, −, × or ÷) were pressed in this sum?

87 ? 19 ? 31 = 2108

6. Which numbers are missing in this calculation?

48 × 7? = ?504

4

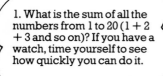

1. What is the sum of all the numbers from 1 to 20 (1 + 2 + 3 and so on)? If you have a watch, time yourself to see how quickly you can do it.

Subtraction puzzles

$$963 - 852 =$$
$$852 - 741 =$$

Try reading the digits on the keyboard downwards and subtracting one column from the next as shown above. What answers do you get?

$$789 - 456 =$$
$$456 - 123 =$$
Try it backwards too
e.g. $987 - 654$.

Now read the digits across and subtract one row from the next. Why do you think the answer is the same in all the sums?

Pairs

$$74 - 47 =$$

7	8	9
4	5	6
1	2	3

$$63 - 36 =$$

$$41 - 14 =$$

Pick any digit on the keyboard and the one below or above it. Reverse the digits to make two numbers, then subtract the smaller from the larger as shown here. Try it several times with different digits and see what happens.

7	8	9
4	5	6
1	2	3

$$69 + 96 = 165$$

$$52 + 25 = 77$$

$$41 + 14 = 55$$

If you add the two numbers the answer is always a multiple of . . . (which number?)

Neighbours

How many of the numbers from 1 to 20 can you make, using only two neighbouring number keys and one operation key, as shown below? You are not allowed to use keys which are diagonal neighbours.

$$\boxed{5} - \boxed{4} = 1 \qquad \boxed{6} \div \boxed{3} = 2 \qquad \boxed{7} - \boxed{4} = 3$$

Which five numbers cannot be made? If you use keys which are diagonal neighbours can you make more of the numbers? How many numbers still cannot be made?

7. Can you work out which numbers are missing in this sum?

$$?3 \times 8? = 7\,??8$$

There are two possible answers. Can you find them both?

Finding out about numbers

Our number system is called a decimal or "base 10" system because it has ten digits (0 1 2 3 4 5 6 7 8 9). Using these ten digits we can make any number including fractions. (This is what makes pocket calculators possible.) For numbers over 9 we use combinations of two or more digits, and we can make any size of number because we can change the value of a digit by changing its position. Look at the numbers below.

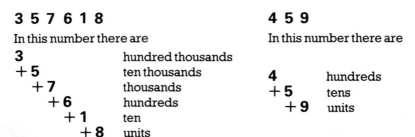

3 5 7 6 1 8

In this number there are

3			hundred thousands
+5			ten thousands
	+7		thousands
	+6		hundreds
		+1	ten
		+8	units

4 5 9

In this number there are

4		hundreds
+5		tens
	+9	units

In the number on the left the figure 5 represents 50 000 and in the righthand number 5 represents 50. Try the puzzle below on a calculator.

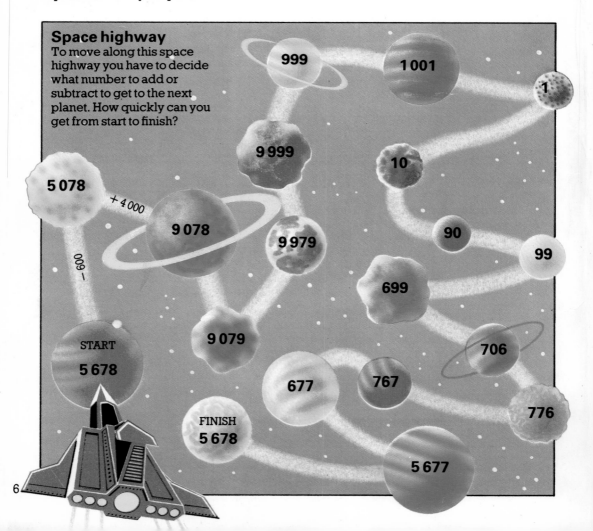

Space highway

To move along this space highway you have to decide what number to add or subtract to get to the next planet. How quickly can you get from start to finish?

999

1 001

1

9 999

10

5 078

+ 4 000

9 078

9 979

90

99

−1 000

699

START
5 678

9 079

677

767

706

FINISH
5 678

776

5 677

6

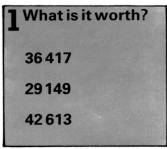

1 What is it worth?

36 417

29 149

42 613

What value does the figure 4 have in each of these numbers?

2

4 762

4 062

What is the difference between these two numbers?

3

472

402

What is the difference between these numbers?

Times by ten

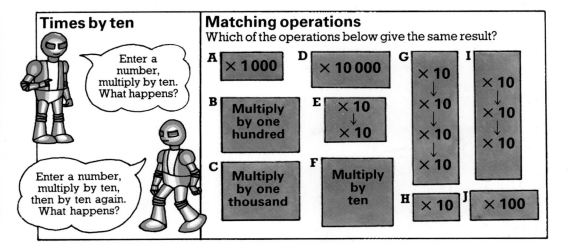

Enter a number, multiply by ten. What happens?

Enter a number, multiply by ten, then by ten again. What happens?

Matching operations

Which of the operations below give the same result?

A × 1 000

B Multiply by one hundred

C Multiply by one thousand

D × 10 000

E × 10 × 10

F Multiply by ten

G × 10 ↓ × 10 ↓ × 10 ↓ × 10

H × 10

I × 10 ↓ × 10 ↓ × 10

J × 100

Give and take game

Here is a game to play with a friend. The aim is to make your calculator display a number larger than a million (1 000 000).

To play, each person enters a six-figure number into their calculator display (each figure should be different). Then they take it in turns to call out a figure between 1 and 9. The value of the figure in the other player's number is added to the caller's own number, and subtracted from the other player's number, as shown in the example below. First over a million wins.

1st player

2nd player

216743

845167

Give me your 6s

You get 60

216803

845107

Give me your 4s

You get nothing

216803

845107

Give me your 7s

Spotting mistakes

It is very easy to press a wrong key on a calculator without realizing it, so you need to be able to recognize when an answer is not correct. The best way to detect errors is to have a rough idea in your head of what the answer should be. The puzzles on these two pages will give you some practice at knowing what answer to expect.

Which is closest?

Without doing the calculations, what size of answers would you expect to the sums below? Choose A, B or C.

1. 97 × 49

A. About 5 000
B. About 2 000
C. About 150

2. 36 912 ÷ 12

A. About   30
B. About   300
C. About 3 000

3. 11 545 − 8 317 + 239 − 1 798

A. Between 10 000 and 11 000
B. Between 3 000 and 4 000
C. Between 1 000 and 2 000

Find the mistakes

The answer 2 961 is correct for only one of these calculations. Can you work out what mistake was made in each of the others?

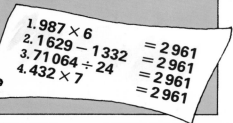

1. 987 × 6   = 2 961
2. 1 629 − 1 332 = 2 961
3. 71 064 ÷ 24   = 2 961
4. 432 × 7   = 2 961

Down to zero

Choose any four-figure number and enter it into your calculator. See if you can reduce the number to zero in exactly four steps. At each step you may only add, subtract, multiply or divide with a two-figure number.

Example ⟶ **5327**

−	2	7	=	**5300**
÷	5	3	=	**100**
−	5	0	=	**50**
−	5	0	=	**0**

Do you think all four-figure numbers can be reduced to zero in four steps?

Race to 1

This is a game for one or two players. Choose any starting number (for example, 28) and enter it. Then choose a key number (for example, 3). Using any operation key but only that key number, see how many steps it takes you to reach 1.

Example ⟶ **28**

+	3	=	**31**
×	3	=	**93**
+	3	=	**96**
+	3	=	**99**
÷	3	3	=	**3**
÷	3	=	**1**

In this example it took six steps to reach 1. Can you do it in less with the same numbers? (It can be done in three steps.)

| Starting number ⟶ | 55 | 40 | 27 |
| Key number ⟶ | **6** | **5** | **7** |

Try the game again with these numbers. If you can get to 1 in eight or nine steps that's good, six or seven is very good and five or less is excellent.

Follow-ons

1. The number 66 can be made by adding four consecutive* numbers. What are they?

2. The number 1 190 is the result of multiplying two consecutive numbers. What are they?

3. The number 504 is the result of multiplying three consecutive numbers. Can you work out what they are?

*Consecutive numbers are ones which directly follow one another e.g. 8, 9, 10.

Reversing puzzle

Enter two digits into the calculator display, the largest first.

`62`

Repeat them to make a six-figure number.

`626262`

Need to subtract
363636

Then work out what number you need to subtract to give an answer which contains the same digits in reverse.

`262626`

Try the puzzle with lots of different pairs of digits. What do you notice about the numbers you have to subtract?

Four-in-a-line game

This game is for two or more players. Take it in turns to choose two numbers from the green panel and multiply them. Then cover the answer on the board below with a coin or a piece of paper. The winner is the first person to cover four numbers in a line.

8	31	12
20	5	71
51	63	22

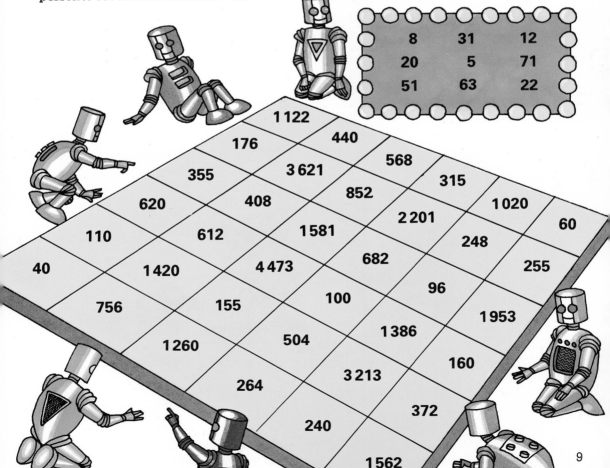

1 122
176   440
355   3 621   568
620   408   852   315
612   1581   2 201   1 020
110   248   60
40   1 420   4 473   682   255
756   155   100   96   1953
1 260   504   1 386   160
264   3 213
372
240
1 562

9

Divisions and decimals

Division trick

Write down a three-figure number. Then enter it twice into a calculator to make a six-figure number in the calculator display.

$$358358$$

Divide by 11, then by 13, then by 7. What happens?

Try the trick with lots of three-figure numbers.

How it works

Repeating the figures of a three-figure number is the same as multiplying it by 1 001.

$$358 \times 1\,001 = 358\,358$$

358 × 1 001 is the same as 358 × 1 000 plus 358 × 1.

Dividing by 11, then 13, then 7 is the same as dividing by 1 001 because 11 × 13 × 7 = 1 001.

$$358\,358 \div 1\,001 = 358$$

The numbers 11, 13 and 7 are called factors of 1 001 because they are whole numbers which, when multiplied together, make 1 001.

Can you think up a four-digit trick which uses the fact that 73 and 137 are factors of 10 001?

Leftovers

If you divide a number by another number which is not one of its factors, the answer will not be a whole number. It can be expressed in several different ways. Look at the example below.

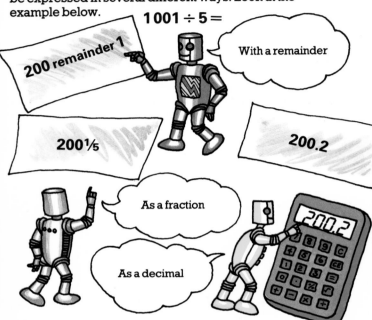

$$1\,001 \div 5 =$$

200 remainder 1

With a remainder

200⅕

200.2

As a fraction

As a decimal

A calculator gives the answer as a decimal. It cannot show remainders or fractions. If a number does not divide exactly, the calculator carries on dividing into the remainder. Can you think of a way to work out the remainder from the calculator's answer? The puzzle below may give you a hint.

Matching puzzle

Can you match these divisions with the answers in the displays? Use a calculator to check your results.

17 ÷ 2

107 ÷ 10

100 ÷ 8

37 ÷ 4

8 ÷ 16

12 ÷ 48

54 ÷ 12

10 ÷ 8

0.5

4.5

10.7

12.5

0.25

8.5

9.25

1.25

Endless answers

20 ÷ 12 = 1.666 666 666 666 666

Often, even the remainder will not divide exactly. This produces a "recurring" decimal in which the numbers after the point are repeated endlessly.

`1.6666667`

Most calculators have space for eight digits in the display, so you never see more than seven of the recurring digits. On some calculators the last digit in the display is rounded off.

More matching puzzles

Here are some more divisions to match with their answers.

30 ÷ 7

26 ÷ 11

10 ÷ 3

17 ÷ 4

5 ÷ 18

9 ÷ 16

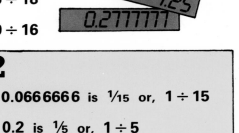

2.3636363
0.5625
4.2857142
3.3333333
4.25
0.2777777

---

1 **Which is bigger?**

0.066 666 6

0.2

Which of these two numbers is bigger? Remember, it is the position of the figures as well as their size, that is important.

2

0.066 666 6 is ¹⁄₁₅ or, 1 ÷ 15

0.2 is ¹⁄₅ or, 1 ÷ 5

In the number 0.066 666 6 the first figure after the decimal point is a zero. In the number 0.2 the first figure after the point is a 2, so 0.2 is the bigger number.

3

AN
AND
ANORAK
ANT
ANTARCTIC
APE
APOCALYPSE

APPROPRIATE
ART
ARTIST
AS

1.89
1.907 3
1.935 2

2.1
2.15
2.166 666
2.25
2.4
2.43

4

2.75
C
2.5
2.474 747 4
2.4
B
2.25
A
2.166 666 6
2.15
2.1

A good way to sort decimal numbers into order of size is to think of them like words in a dictionary. For example, AN comes before APOCALYPSE because N comes before P in the alphabet.

These cards are in numerical order. The three blank cards hold the answers to the calculations 7 ÷ 3, 49 ÷ 19 and 440 ÷ 200. Can you work out which calculation belongs to which card?

11

Fraction puzzles

To work out fractions on a calculator you have to convert them to decimals by dividing the top part by the bottom part as shown below.

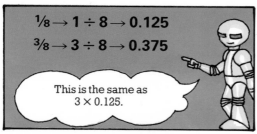

$$\tfrac{1}{8} \rightarrow 1 \div 8 \rightarrow 0.125$$
$$\tfrac{3}{8} \rightarrow 3 \div 8 \rightarrow 0.375$$

This is the same as 3×0.125.

Some fractions produce interesting results. Try $\tfrac{1}{3}$, $\tfrac{2}{3}$ and $\tfrac{3}{3}$.

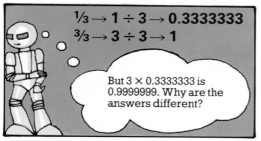

$$\tfrac{1}{3} \rightarrow 1 \div 3 \rightarrow 0.3333333$$
$$\tfrac{3}{3} \rightarrow 3 \div 3 \rightarrow 1$$

But 3×0.3333333 is 0.9999999. Why are the answers different?

The reason for the different answers is that 0.3333333 is not exactly $\tfrac{1}{3}$, but it is the nearest you can get on a calculator. When it is multiplied by 3 the answer is very close to, but not exactly, 1.

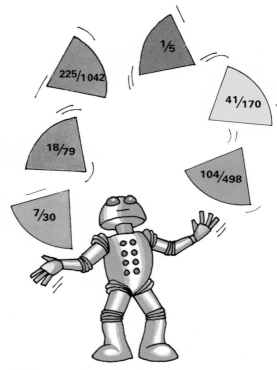

$\tfrac{225}{1042}$ $\tfrac{1}{5}$ $\tfrac{41}{170}$ $\tfrac{18}{79}$ $\tfrac{104}{498}$ $\tfrac{7}{30}$

Sizing up fractions

It is often very difficult to know whether one fraction is bigger than another, especially when they have different figures at the bottom. If you convert the fractions to decimals it is much easier to tell. Can you arrange the above fractions in order of size, smallest first?

Triad
This is a game to play with a friend. You need a piece of paper and two different coloured pens or pencils.

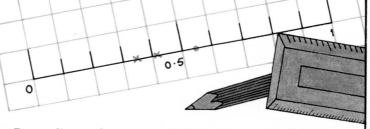

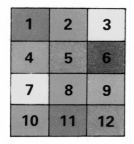

1	2	3
4	5	6
7	8	9
10	11	12

Draw a line on the paper and divide it into tenths. Label the ends of the line 0 and 1 and the centre-point 0.5.

To play the game each player in turn chooses two numbers from the chart on the left to make a fraction, then converts it to a decimal and marks its place on the line. The aim of the game is to get three marks on the line without any of your opponent's marks in between.

If the decimal equivalent of your fraction is more than 1, your mark goes off the line and you miss a go.

Lost fraction puzzle

I divided two whole numbers under 20 and got this answer. Now I have forgotten what the numbers were. Can you work them out?

0.2307692

1 Finding patterns

$\frac{1}{7}$ $\frac{2}{7}$ $\frac{3}{7}$

$\frac{4}{7}$ $\frac{5}{7}$ $\frac{6}{7}$

If you convert sevenths fractions to decimals you get the same pattern of digits starting in a different place in each answer. Try converting the sevenths shown above and see if you recognize the pattern.

Tops and bottoms

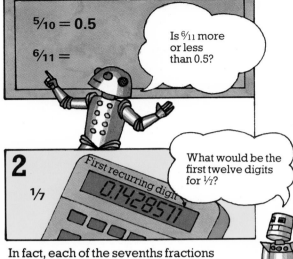

$\frac{5}{10} = 0.5$

$\frac{6}{11} =$

Is $\frac{6}{11}$ more or less than 0.5?

What would be the first twelve digits for $\frac{1}{7}$?

2

$\frac{1}{7}$

First recurring digit
0.1428571

In fact, each of the sevenths fractions produces a recurring decimal in which a pattern of six digits repeats itself. Most calculator displays only have room to show the pattern once but you can see the first recurring digit.

3

$\frac{1}{17} = 0.058\,823\,5$

$\frac{2}{17} = 0.117\,647\,0$

$\frac{3}{17} = 0.176\,470\,5$

$\frac{4}{17} = 0.235\,294\,1$

$\frac{5}{17} = 0.294\,117\,6$

$\frac{6}{17} =$

Seventeenths fractions produce a recurring pattern with sixteen digits. This is much too long for a calculator to display. Can you find the pattern from the conversions shown above and work out all sixteen recurring digits for $\frac{1}{17}$?

Try to predict the decimal value of $\frac{6}{17}$ without using a calculator.

Can you find any other interesting patterns when converting fractions to decimals? Elevenths and thirteenths are good ones to try.

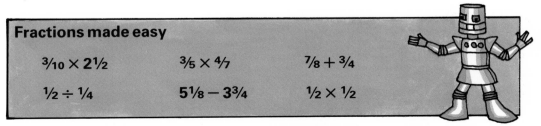

Fractions made easy

$\frac{3}{10} \times 2\frac{1}{2}$ $\frac{3}{5} \times \frac{4}{7}$ $\frac{7}{8} + \frac{3}{4}$

$\frac{1}{2} \div \frac{1}{4}$ $5\frac{1}{8} - 3\frac{3}{4}$ $\frac{1}{2} \times \frac{1}{2}$

Calculations with fractions are much easier to do using a calculator. You just change the fractions to decimals before you start. Try these examples.

To save writing down the decimal equivalents of the fractions, you could store one of them in the memory while you work out the other.

13

Being too accurate

With an eight-digit display calculators are often much more accurate than you need. For instance, say you wanted to find out how long it would take to travel a journey of 270km at 110km/h.

270 ÷ 110 = 2.454 545 4 hours

The calculator's answer is not a very useful reply to the question because it is too detailed. To plan the journey all you need to know is that it would take roughly two and a half hours. So rounding off 2.454 545 4 to 2.5 is accurate enough for this particular question.

When you solve a problem you should think about how accurate you need to be to give an answer which is meaningful for the question. How would you round off the numbers in the statements below if you were telling them to a friend?

1. A light year is 5 865 696 000 000 miles or 9 385 113 600 000 kilometres.

2. There are 30 126 541 cats in the USA.

3. The population of London is 6 877 142.

4. The shortest street in Britain is 17.672 metres long.

Puzzles

1. The world speed record for the fastest train is 410 kilometres per hour. In 1829 the record was 29.1 miles per hour. How many times greater is the new record? (1 mile is ⁸⁄₅ kilometres.)

2. The longest railway line in the world stretches 9 438km from Moscow to Nakhodka. How long would it take a train travelling at an average speed of 120km/h to complete the journey?

> 3. Have you lived a million hours?

Three-figure accuracy

To round off the distance 293 467km to the nearest ten thousand kilometres gives 290 000km. Only the first two figures in the number are accurate and these are called the significant figures.

As a general rule an answer with *three* significant figures is accurate enough for most problems. Rounding a number to three significant figures means you are ignoring a very small part of the answer. You can see this in the example below.

293 467 becomes **293 000**

The error is **467** in **293 000** or ⁴⁶⁷⁄₂₉₃ ₀₀₀

That is about ⁵⁰⁰⁄₃₀₀ ₀₀₀ or ¹⁄₆₀₀.

Rounding the distance 293 467km to three significant figures gives an error of 467 in 293 000 or about 1 in 600, so you are only ignoring one six-hundredth of the answer.

Hints for rounding off

1. The zeros between the significant figures and the decimal point do not count.

0.005 213 3 → 0.005 21

26 833 000 → 26 800 000

2. If the fourth figure is a 5 or above you should add 1 to the third significant figure.

0.005 216 → 0.005 22

543.724 → 544

> Can you round these answers to three significant figures?
>
> 1. **0.006 376 3**
> 2. **0.062 871 9**
> 3. **264.374 12**
> 4. **781 432.16**
> 5. **0.199 999 9**

Space puzzles

When you do these puzzles, round off the answers so they are meaningful to you.

1. The Moon is 240 000 miles away. How long would a spaceship take to travel to the Moon at 1 mile per second?

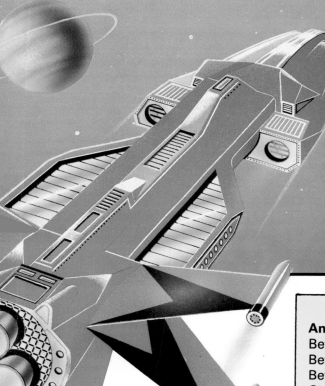

2. A spaceship leaves Earth and travels at 40 000km/h. How long will it take to reach Mars which is 56 million km away?

3. The Sun and the Moon appear about the same size. But the diameter of the Sun is 1 382 400km and the diameter of the Moon is only 3 480km. How many times wider is the Sun than the Moon really?

SCOREBOARD

Answer	Score
Between 0 and 1	1 point
Between 1 and 10	2 points
Between 10 and 100	3 points
Over 100	zero

CHART

9	23	31	46
97	129	152	216
255	364	440	800
1 974	2 132	2 561	2 619
2 815	3 966	4 770	9 342
13 000	14 500	16 000	29 500

In-between game

To play this game you need two people. Take turns to choose two numbers from the chart on the right. Divide one by the other, then check the scoreboard to see how many points you have scored. The first player to score 10 points wins. (A number cannot be used twice in one game.)

Use your memory

The memory on a calculator is very useful when you are doing calculations with several parts. The labels on the memory keys vary from one calculator to another and if yours are different from the ones shown here check your instruction manual.

To store a number in the memory you use the M+ key. On many calculators you erase a number from the memory by pressing the MR (memory recall) key twice. On others you press MR to display the number, then M− to subtract the number in the display from the one in the memory.

Try these calculations to practise using the memory keys.

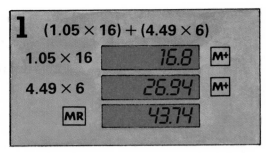

To work out this sum you do the first multiplication and store the answer in the memory. Then do the second multiplication and add the result to the memory by pressing the M+ key. The memory now holds the total of both sums. To display it press the MR key.

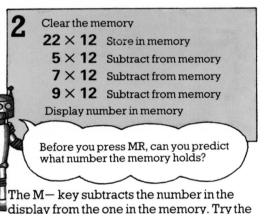

Before you press MR, can you predict what number the memory holds?

The M− key subtracts the number in the display from the one in the memory. Try the above routine to practise using it. Leave the final answer in the memory so you can use it in the next routine.

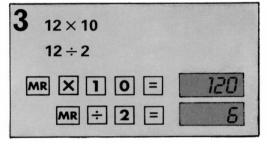

Once a number is stored in the memory you can use it for lots of separate calculations. Try the examples above. Using the number in new calculations does not wipe it from the memory. It is only removed if you erase it or switch the calculator off.

Repeats

Here are some calculations which produce interesting number patterns. Each one involves using a number over and over again and you could store that number in the memory.

See if you can work out why the patterns occur. There are some hints with the answers at the back of the book.

Conversions

85km	100km	50km	270km
126km	32km	10km	115km

Can you convert these distances in kilometres to miles? (A kilometre is ⅝ of a mile.) Try using the memory to speed up the calculations.

Order of calculations

When you are using the memory to work out divisions you have to plan the calculation carefully. Look at the example below.

$$\frac{285 + 117}{264 - 68}$$

1. $264 - 68 =$ M+

2. $285 + 117 =$

3. ÷ MR =

Do the sum in this order.

To do this calculation you need to work out the bottom part first and store the result in the memory. Then work out the top part and divide this answer by the number in the memory. For more practice with calculations like this try the planet puzzle on page 18.

Who wins?

Can you solve this puzzle? You need to plan the calculation carefully so you can use the memory on your calculator. The horse can run a mile in 1 minute and 35 seconds, and the woman can run 800 metres in 1 minute 44 seconds. If the woman is given a 1 000 yards start, who will win the mile race?

Hints for working it out

You need to work out the woman's running speed in metres per second, and you will also have to convert the distance she still has to run into metres.
(1 mile = 1 760 yards and 1 yard = 0.9144 metres.)

Upside-down planet puzzle

You are the commander of a spaceship which is on a reconnaissance mission of a group of planets. Coded instructions for where to go next are hidden in mathematical calculations which you are given each time you reach a planet. To read the instructions you need to work out the calculations and then decode the answer. Starting from Earth what is the final message you receive?

LESBOS

Next go to

$$5\,000 \times \left[\frac{47\,512.562}{803.5 \times 4} \right]$$

ISIS

SIBEL

Next

$$\frac{95\,380\,000 + 8\,706}{193 \times 7}$$

Next

$$\frac{96.47 + 4\,998.9}{0.007\,64 - 0.001 + 0.003\,36}$$

LILOSI

Fly to

$$\frac{8.3844}{20.63 - 6.93}$$

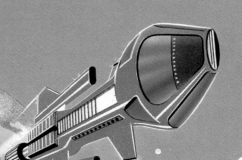

Go to

$$\frac{152\,139}{48.54 + 167.26}$$

EARTH

SOL

Next visit

$$\frac{8\,515\,510.5}{2\,647.64 - 2\,591.14}$$

Now

$$\frac{141.064\,27}{157.8 \div 789}$$

GOGOL

ZIGO

Full speed now to

$$\frac{1717 \times 441}{37\,191 \div 253}$$

Constant calculations

The constant function on a calculator is a kind of automatic memory. It allows you to repeat a function and number without re-entering them. Not all calculators have a constant function. To check whether yours has, try this test.

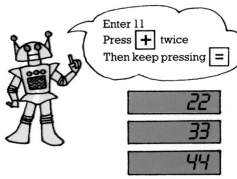

Enter 11
Press $+$ twice
Then keep pressing $=$

	22
	33
	44

If your calculator has a constant function it will add 11 every time you press the = key. Some calculators have a constant which works automatically, so you need only press the + key once.

Investigating constants

If your calculator has a constant function, try these.

1. 0 $\cdot$ 5 $+$ $+$ $=$

2. 1 0 $\times$ $\times$ $=$

3. 5 $-$ $-$ $=$

4. 1 $\div$ $\div$ $=$

5. 1 $\cdot$ 5 $\times$ $\times$ $=$

Which brings you closest to 100, ten presses or eleven?

6. $-$ 5 $-$ $-$ $=$

Why does this get bigger?

7. 9 $\times$ $\times$ $=$ or 9 $+$ $+$ $=$

Which of these would you press to get all the multiples of 9 in the nine-times-table?

1 Using the constant

$60 \div 5$
$5\,000 \div 5$
$12.5 \div 5$
$0.5 \div 5$

Try these. To put "÷ 5" in the constant press
5 $\div$ $\div$ *

Once you have given the calculator a constant such as "÷ 5", you can use it on any number you enter, so long as you do not clear the display or press an operation key.

2

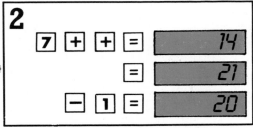

7 $+$ $+$ $=$	14
$=$	21
$-$ 1 $=$	20

If you want to do a different calculation with a number which appears in the display, you can do so because pressing any operation key will cancel the constant.

3

$+$ 1 0 K $=$	20
$=$	30
$=$	40

Some calculators, particularly scientific ones, have a constant key labelled K. To use the constant you enter the function and number you want to repeat, then press K, as shown above.

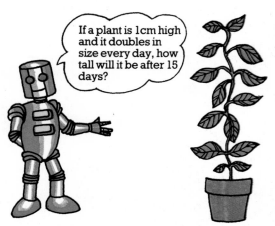

If a plant is 1cm high and it doubles in size every day, how tall will it be after 15 days?

*On calculators with an automatic constant you may need to press the 5, ÷ and = keys before starting.

Percentage puzzles

The island of Brigg has a population of 249 000. If 20% of the population emigrate, how many people leave the island?

> To work out percentages you multiply the number by the percentage you want and press the % key. There is no need to press =.

The number of people left is now 80% of the original population. How many people is that? Can you think of a way to check the answer?

| 20% of 4 000 | 20% of 12.5 | 90% of 8.9 | 50% of 500 |

Can you work out these percentages?

More about percentages

> A percentage is a useful way to describe a fraction of something. For instance, 20% is the same as ⅕ and 75% is the same as ¾.

75%

20%

> Like fractions, percentages can be expressed as decimals.

$20\% \rightarrow {}^{20}/_{100} \rightarrow {}^{1}/_{5} \rightarrow 0.2$

$75\% \rightarrow {}^{75}/_{100} \rightarrow {}^{3}/_{4} \rightarrow 0.75$

Percentage chart

%	FRACTION (OVER 100)	SIMPLE FRACTION	DECIMAL
50%	$\frac{50}{100}$		0·5
25%	$\frac{25}{100}$		
10%		$\frac{1}{10}$	
33⅓%	$\frac{33\cdot33}{100}$	$\frac{1}{3}$	0·3333
15%		$\frac{3}{20}$	
		$\frac{2}{3}$	

Percentages without a % key

> 20% of 249 000 is the same as 249 000 × 0.2. See if you can work out the examples below without using the percentage key.

15% of 30

50% of 50

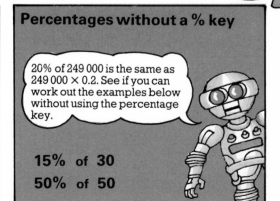

The chart above shows the most commonly used percentages with their fraction and decimal equivalents. Can you fill in the missing numbers?

If your calculator does not have a percentage key, you will need to convert percentages to decimals to work them out. To do this you divide by 100 as shown in the chart on the left.

What's the difference?

If the weight of an astronaut from Earth increases by 20% on planet Zardoz, how much would you weigh on Zardoz? You can work this out in six different ways, as shown below. Methods 1, 2 and 3 give the percentage increase, which you then add on to your weight. Methods 4, 5 and 6 give the new weight direct.

1. Multiply weight by 20%.
2. Multiply weight by 20 and divide by 100.
3. Multiply weight by 0.2.
4. Multiply weight by 120%.
5. Multiply weight by 120 and divide by 100.
6. Multiply weight by 1.2.

Half-life

The radioactive output of an imaginary chemical, Zilium, is 463 units, but it decreases by 50% every day. How many days will it take for the radioactive output to be within the "safe" level of 4 units?

Orang-utan puzzle

The orang-utan is in danger of extinction. If there are 5 000 left in the wild now and their numbers decreased by 15% each year, how many years would it be before there are less than 2 500?

Prize money puzzle

You have won a TV quiz, but there is one final question: how do you want to receive the money? There are two choices.

1. You can have 100 banknotes the first year, 10% less the next year, 10% less the year after and so on for ten years.

2. You can have 10 banknotes the first year, 50% more the year after and so on for ten years.

Which method would you choose? (You could use the memory on your calculator to keep a running total of the amounts you get each year.)

Square numbers

Squaring a number means multiplying it by itself. For example, seven squared (written 7^2) is 7×7. The square of 7 is therefore 49.

Small square numbers are easy to calculate in your head but you need to use a calculator to find larger squares.

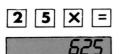

$$625$$

$$6.25$$

On most calculators you can use the constant function to square a number. *

Some calculators have a squaring key marked x^2. This will give you the square of any number you enter.

1 Square number puzzles

12^2 21^2 113^2 311^2 1003^2 3001^2 201^2 102^2

These pairs of square numbers produce interesting results when you work them out. See if you can find any others like them.

2

$$1^2 =$$
$$11^2 =$$
$$111^2 =$$
$$1111^2 =$$

Here are some more squares to investigate. What pattern of answers do they produce?

3

$$5^2 =$$
$$15^2 =$$
$$25^2 =$$
$$35^2 =$$
$$45^2 =$$

Work out these squares and write down the answers. Then see if you can work out the square of 55 without using a calculator (or pencil and paper).

4

$$1301 = ?^2 + ?^2$$

The figure 1 301 is the sum of the squares of two consecutive numbers. Can you calculate what they are?

5

$$3^2 + 6^2 + 7^2 = 2^2 + 3^2 + 9^2$$

Is this true?

All these equations are different combinations of the same numbers. Which of them do you think are true?

1. $32^2 + 63^2 + 79^2 = 23^2 + 36^2 + 97^2$

2. $33^2 + 69^2 + 72^2 = 33^2 + 96^2 + 27^2$

3. $32^2 + 69^2 + 73^2 = 23^2 + 96^2 + 37^2$

4. $39^2 + 62^2 + 73^2 = 93^2 + 26^2 + 37^2$

5. $39^2 + 63^2 + 72^2 = 93^2 + 36^2 + 27^2$

6. $33^2 + 62^2 + 79^2 = 33^2 + 26^2 + 97^2$

*You will probably only need to press the $\times$ key once.

Ancient triangles

Measurements at prehistoric sites, such as Stonehenge in England, show that Stone Age builders had discovered the principles of Pythagoras' theorem long before Pythagoras was born.

A theorem is a mathematical statement which can be proved to be true.

Pythagoras' theorem states that whenever a triangle has a square corner (that is, a right-angle of 90°), the square of the longest side is equal to the sum of the squares of the other two sides. You can check this on the triangle shown above.

The theorem also works the other way round. If the squares of two sides of a triangle equal the square of the third side, the triangle must contain a right-angle. Is the above triangle right-angled?

3, 4, 5   **12, 35, 37**   **5, 12, 13**   **19, 59, 62**

41, 71, 82   **8, 15, 17**   **8, 9, 12**

The Stone Age builders used triangles in order to construct right-angled corners. However they were not always absolutely accurate. The measurements above are from triangles found in Stonehenge and other sites. Which ones give perfect right-angles?

Pythagoras puzzles

Pythagoras' theorem is also useful for calculating an unknown distance. For instance, what is the length of the third side in this right-angled triangle?

What about the one on the right?

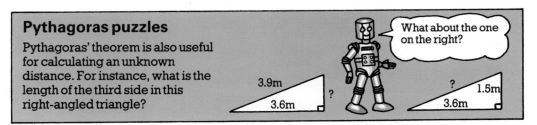

Opposites

Some operations on a calculator have the opposite, or inverse, effect of one another. For example, dividing by 3 reverses the effect of multiplying by 3. Look at the example on the right.

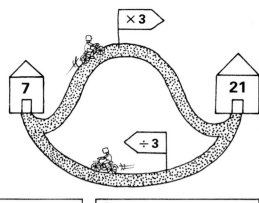

Now try these.

1

The four basic operations on a calculator can be divided into two pairs of inverses. Which are the pairs?

2

× 12
+ 17
− 7
÷ 10

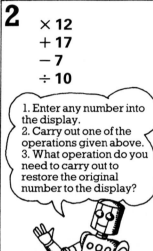

1. Enter any number into the display.
2. Carry out one of the operations given above.
3. What operation do you need to carry out to restore the original number to the display?

Try the robot's routine above to find the inverses of each of the operations at the top of the box.

3

The operation ÷ 3 reverses the effect of × 3, but does × 3 reverse ÷ 3? Try it on several different numbers and see.

Alternatives

There is usually more than one inverse for a particular operation. For example if you multiply by 2, you can get back to the original number by ÷ 2 or × 0.5.

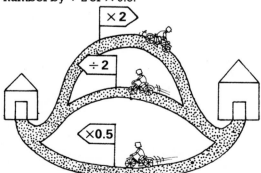

Can you find more than one inverse of the operation ÷ 0.5?

Inverses puzzle

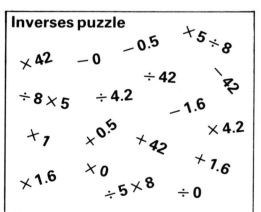

× 42   − 0   − 0.5   × 5 ÷ 8

÷ 42

÷ 8 × 5   ÷ 4.2   − 42

− 1.6

× 1   + 0.5   × 4.2

× 1.6   × 0   + 42   + 1.6

÷ 5 × 8   ÷ 0

From the operations shown above, how many pairs can you make in which one operation is the inverse of the other? Which operations are left over?

Square roots

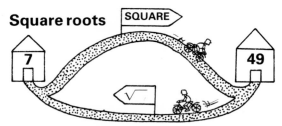

Finding a square root is the inverse of squaring. The square root of 49 (written $\sqrt{49}$) is 7.

Some calculators have a square root key labelled $\sqrt{}$. You can see how to use it above.

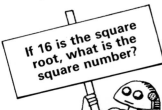

If 16 is the square root, what is the square number?

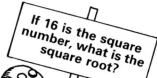

If 16 is the square number, what is the square root?

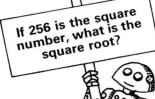

If 256 is the square number, what is the square root?

Square roots without a $\sqrt{}$ key

Finding a square root without a square root key is a matter of trial and error. For example to find $\sqrt{70}$ first make a guess.

$8^2 = 64$ and $9^2 = 81$, so try 8.5^2.

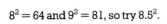
72.25

Too big, try 8.4^2.

70.56

Still too big, try 8.3^2.

68.89

What would you try next?

Can you continue the calculation to find the square root of 70 correct to three decimal places (i.e. your answer should show three figures after the decimal point)?

In fact a calculator also works out square roots by trial and error, and some calculators take longer to display square roots than other answers.

Square root trick

To do this mind-reading trick ask a friend to think of two numbers with a difference of 2 between them (e.g. 16 and 18) and to remember them without telling you what they are. Then give your friend a calculator and the following instructions:

Multiply the two ———— 1 6 ×
numbers.
1 8 =

Then add 1. ———— + 1 =

Now take the ———— 289
calculator and find
the square root of
the number in the
display. √

17

Adding 1 to this result will give you one of the numbers your friend thought of and subtracting 1 from it will give the other. Try the trick with lots of different numbers.

Circular calculations

People have known for a long time that, no matter what the size of a circle, its circumference is always "three and a bit" times longer than its diameter. However the exact size of the "bit" has not been found. The number "three and a bit" is represented by the Greek letter π (pronounced pie). Modern computers have calculated the value of π to several thousand decimal places. The first six hundred are shown below.

$\pi =$ 3.14159265358979323846264338329750288419716939
9375105820974944592307816406286208998628034825342
11706798214808651328230664709384460955058223172 53
59408128481117450284102701938521105559644622948 95
49303819644288109756659334461284756482337867831 65
27120190914564856692346034861045432664821339360 72
60249141273724587006606315588174881520920962822 95
40917153643678925903600113305305488204665213841 46
95194151160943305727036575959195309218611738193 26
11793105118548074462379962749567351885752724891 22
79381830119491298336733624406566430860021394946395
22473719070217986094370277053921717629317675238 46
74818467669405132

Over the centuries, different mathematicians have suggested various values for π. Some of these are shown below. Which one is closest to the computer's figure?

$4 \times (1 - \frac{1}{9})^2$ ◀— Egyptian (1650 BC)

$3\frac{1}{8}$ ◀— Babylonian (before 500 BC)

$\sqrt{2} + \sqrt{3}$ ◀— Greek (450 BC)

$355/113$ ◀— Chinese (AD 500)

$3927/1250$ ◀— Indian (AD 400)

Between $3\frac{1}{7}$ and $3^{10}/_{71}$ ◀— Archimedes (220 BC)

Using π

Knowing the value of π enables you to calculate the curved distance around a circle or sphere (that is, its circumference). For instance, this can has a diameter of 12cm, and its circumference is $\pi \times 12$.

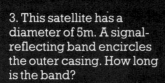

If your calculator has a key which displays the number π you can work out the answer as shown above. (If not, enter a rounded-off version of π, e.g. 3.142.) The can would need a label 37.7cm long to go right round it. How long would the label for a can with a 16cm diameter need to be?

Earth puzzles

1. The diameter of the Earth is 12 640km, how long is its circumference?

2. If a satellite orbits Earth at an altitude of 100km, what is the length of its orbit?

3. This satellite has a diameter of 5m. A signal-reflecting band encircles the outer casing. How long is the band?

4. If the band were mounted 1m from the surface of the satellite how much longer would it have to be?

5. Imagine a rope long enough to go right round the Equator. How much longer would it have to be to encircle the Equator at a height of 1m from its surface? (The diameter of the Earth is 12 640 000m.)

6. A spaceship orbiting the Moon (diameter 3 480km) completes an orbit in eight hours. If its speed is 1 680km/h how far does it travel in one orbit? How far away from the Moon is its orbit?

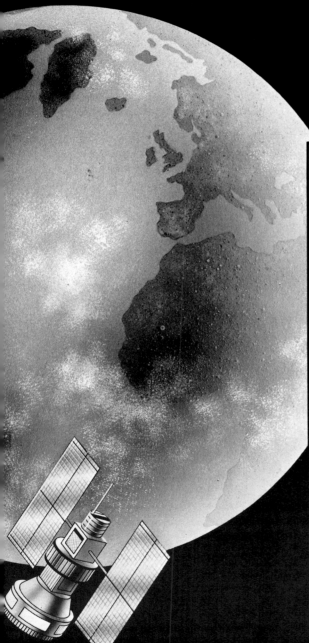

Division puzzle

How good is your division? This puzzle will test your skill. In the number below all the digits are different.

38 125

The first digit, 3, can be divided exactly by 1.
The first two digits, 38, can be divided exactly by 2.
The first three digits, 381, can be divided exactly by 3.
The first four digits, 3 812, can be divided exactly by 4.
The first five digits, 38 125, can be divided exactly by 5.

Can you make up a five-digit number starting with 7 in which the digits work like this? (All the digits must be different.) Get a friend to check your answer.

Can you make up a six-digit or a seven-digit number like it?

There is one nine-digit number which works in the same way. Can you work out what it is?

Large number problems

Some problems involve numbers which are too big for a calculator to display. Most scientific calculators have a system called "scientific notation" for dealing with large numbers (pages 34-35) but here is a way of coping with them on simple calculators.

Adding and subtracting large numbers

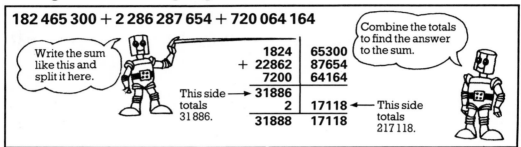

182 465 300 + 2 286 287 654 + 720 064 164

Write the sum like this and split it here.

Combine the totals to find the answer to the sum.

	1824	65300
+	22862	87654
	7200	64164
This side totals 31 886.	31886	
	2	17118
	31888	**17118**

This side totals 217 118.

To add numbers which will not fit into the display, you can split the sum as shown above and add each side separately. Then combine the answers. Remember to carry a number from the righthand total across to the left if necessary.

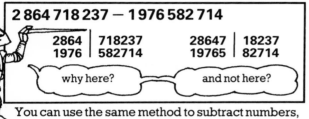

2 864 718 237 − 1 976 582 714

2864	718237		28647	18237
1976	582714		19765	82714

why here? and not here?

You can use the same method to subtract numbers, but you have to be careful where you split the sum. Why would you split the above subtraction in the position shown on the left?

Examples to try

1.   5 266 834 710
  +   276 647 433
    27 164 311 803

How would you do this sum?

2.   980 065 432
  − 735 917 141

3.   1 262 587 652 321 987 125
  +   921 766 412 005 286 421

Multiplications and divisions

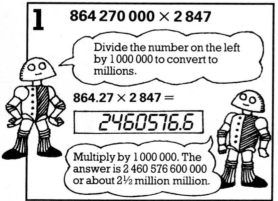

1   **864 270 000 × 2 847**

Divide the number on the left by 1 000 000 to convert to millions.

864.27 × 2 847 =

```
2460576.6
```

Multiply by 1 000 000. The answer is 2 460 576 600 000 or about 2½ million million.

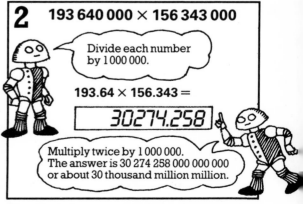

2   **193 640 000 × 156 343 000**

Divide each number by 1 000 000.

193.64 × 156.343 =

```
30274.258
```

Multiply twice by 1 000 000. The answer is 30 274 258 000 000 000 or about 30 thousand million million.

The trick for doing multiplications and divisions is to convert the numbers to millions and compensate for this afterwards. To convert numbers to millions you move the decimal point six places to the left (i.e. divide by 1 000 000).

If both numbers are too big for the display you have to convert them both to millions and then multiply the answer by a million million to compensate (move the decimal point twelve places to the right).

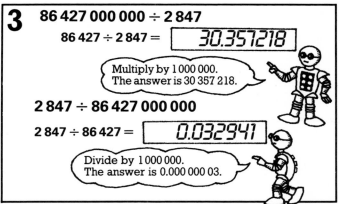

3 86 427 000 000 ÷ 2 847

86 427 ÷ 2 847 = `30.357218`

Multiply by 1 000 000.
The answer is 30 357 218.

2 847 ÷ 86 427 000 000

2 847 ÷ 86 427 = `0.032941`

Divide by 1 000 000.
The answer is 0.000 000 03.

In divisions with big numbers the way you compensate the answer depends on which number in the sum you converted to millions. Decide what size of answer you would expect and then multiply or divide the calculator's answer accordingly.

4 86 427 000 000 ÷ 288 090 000

86 427 ÷ 288.09 = `300`

This is the correct answer.

If you convert both numbers in a division to millions the answer the calculator gives is correct.

Overflows

456 000 × 123 000

`560.88000E`

The E shows that the decimal point should be eight places to the right, so the correct answer is 56 088 000 000.

Some calculators have an "overflow check" and display an E if an answer is too large for the display. Try the example above. If your calculator displays an E you can find the right answer by moving the decimal point eight places to the right.

The overflow check prevents any further calculations with that number. However on some calculators you can release the overflow check by pressing "clear entry" and continue calculating. Remember to move the decimal point eight places to the right in your final answer.

Famous chessboard problem

The story is told of an Indian philosopher who helped his ruler in a time of great difficulty and was offered anything he wanted as a reward. The philosopher said he simply wanted 1 grain of rice on the first square of a chessboard, two grains on the second, four on the third, eight on the fourth and so on, for each square doubling the number on the previous square. The ruler laughed and was pleased that he did not have to part with any of his riches, but he soon stopped laughing. Use the constant function (2 × × =, or 2 × =) to find out why.

Sums inside sums

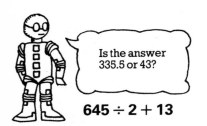

Is the answer 335.5 or 43?

$645 \div 2 + 13$

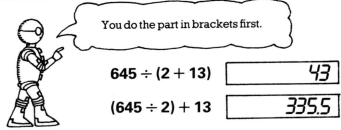

You do the part in brackets first.

$645 \div (2 + 13)$ — `43`

$(645 \div 2) + 13$ — `335.5`

This calculation has two possible answers depending on whether you do the division or the addition first.

To avoid confusion in calculations with several parts, mathematicians use brackets to show which part should be done first. Many scientific calculators have brackets keys and automatically work out calculations in the correct order.

Examples

1. $41 - (32 - 21)$
2. $117 + (39 \div 3)$
3. $(121 \div 11) - 10$
4. $19 + (348 \div 16)$
5. $(200 - 135) \div 45$
6. $(47 - 7) \div (100 \div 5)$

$135 \div 15 - 6 + 5$

`20`

`-2`

`8`

Try these calculations. If your calculator has brackets keys you can enter them as they are written. If it does not you need to decide the order. (You could use the memory to store the answer to one part while you do the other.)

Where would you put the brackets in this calculation to give the different answers shown above?

Calculating Easter

The date of Easter varies from year to year and is calculated from the phases of the Moon. (The Sun, Moon and Earth are lined up only once every 19 years. The intervening years are called the 19 phases of the Moon.) The calculation to find the date of Easter Saturday is shown below. It is quite long with lots of separate stages. The letters represent the answers and the remainders you get at each stage. To start the calculation you only need to know Y (the year). See if you can calculate when Easter will fall next year.*

$Y \div 19 = Z$, remainder A ← This division is to find out which phase the Moon is in.

$Y \div 100 = B$, remainder C ← This is to find out which century the year is in . .

$B \div 4 = D$, remainder E ←

$(B + 8) \div 25 = F$, remainder G

$(B + 1 - F) \div 3 = H$, remainder I   . . . and these two are to check for leap years.

$(19 \times A) + (B + 15) - (D + H) = J$

$J \div 30 = K$, remainder L

$C \div 4 = M$, remainder N

$(2 \times E) + (2 \times M) + 32 - (L + N) = P$

$P \div 7 = Q$, remainder R

$A + (11 \times L) + (22 \times R) = S$

$S \div 451 = T$, remainder U

$(L + R + 114) - (7 \times T) = V$

$V \div 31 = W$, remainder X

30   W is the month, X the day and Y the year.

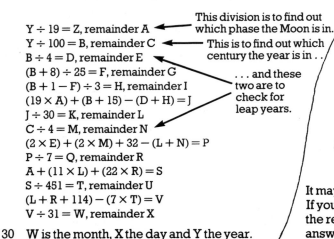

$Y = 1990$

REMAINDERS

$Z = 104$ $A = 14$

$B = 19$ $C = 90$

$D = 4$

$E = 3$

It may help to make a chart like this. If you are not sure how to work out the remainder from the calculator's answer, see Leftovers on page 43.

*You can check your answer in a diary.

Brackets inside brackets

1. $10 \div (10 \div (10 \div (10 \div (10 \div 10))))$

2. $10 \times [10 \div (10 \times \{10 \div [10 \times (10 \div 10)]\})]$

3. $$\frac{1}{\left(1 + \left(\frac{1}{\left(1 + \left(\frac{1}{(1+1)}\right)\right)}\right)\right)}$$ ← Press the "close brackets" key five times before you press =.

Press the "close brackets" key four times at the end, before you press =.
Sometimes different pairs of brackets are written differently, but they are all the same to a calculator.

Can you unravel these calculations? The rule for working out brackets inside brackets (nested brackets) is to do the sum in the innermost brackets first and work outwards. On a calculator with brackets keys you can enter the calculations in the order they are written, because when you press the "open brackets" key the calculator will not do the sum inside until you press the "close brackets" key.

Reciprocals

A reciprocal is a number divided into 1, so ⅓ is the reciprocal of 3 and ⅕ is the reciprocal of 5. Reciprocals are simply fractions where the top part is 1 (called unit fractions) but they occur so frequently in calculations that many scientific calculators have a key for working them out. The reciprocal key divides any number you enter into 1 and expresses its reciprocal as a decimal. You can see how to use it on the right.

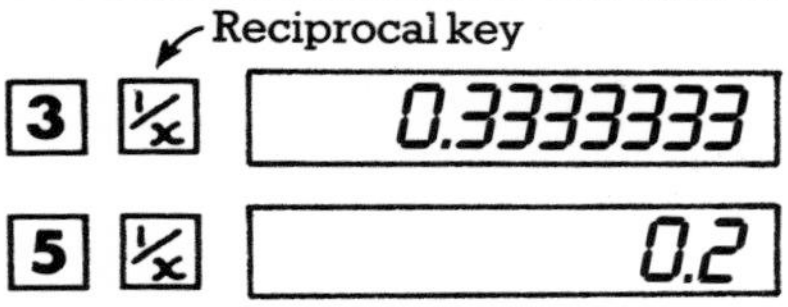

Reciprocal key
3 1/x 0.3333333
5 1/x 0.2

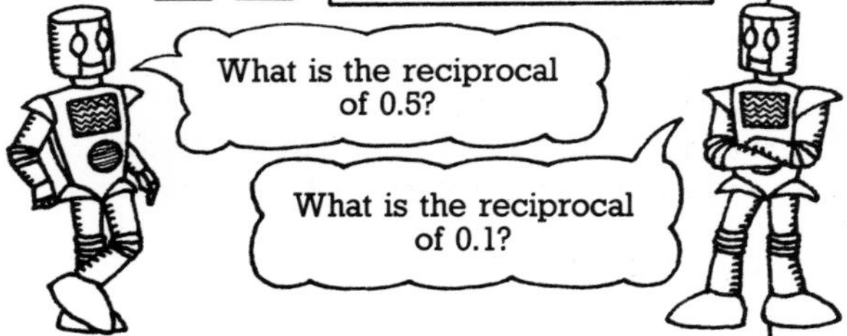

What is the reciprocal of 0.5?
What is the reciprocal of 0.1?

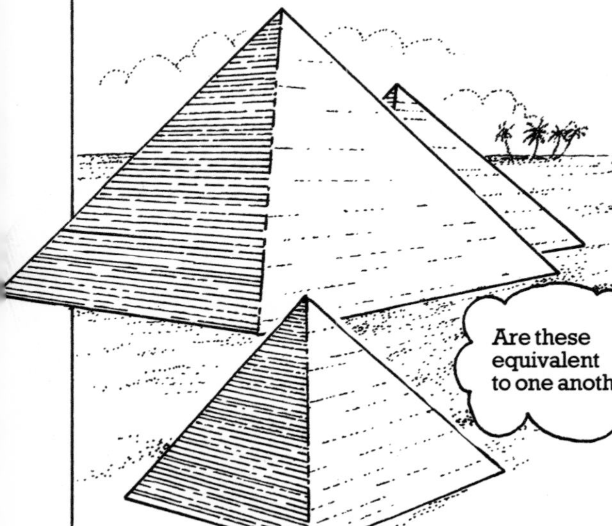

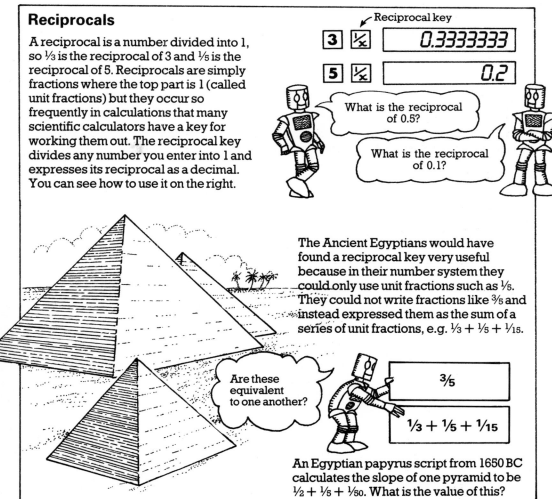

The Ancient Egyptians would have found a reciprocal key very useful because in their number system they could only use unit fractions such as ⅕. They could not write fractions like ⅗ and instead expressed them as the sum of a series of unit fractions, e.g. ⅓ + ⅕ + 1/15.

Are these equivalent to one another?
3/5
1/3 + 1/5 + 1/15

An Egyptian papyrus script from 1650 BC calculates the slope of one pyramid to be ½ + ⅕ + 1/50. What is the value of this?

Power puzzles

The solution to the chessboard problem on page 29 involved multiplying 2 by 2 by 2 by 2 . . . a total of 63 times. Mathematicians write this as 2^{63} (2 to the power of 63).

Powers on a calculator

  $7^2 \; 2^{14} \; 2^{15} \; 2^{30}$

On a scientific calculator you can use the power key, marked y^x, to multiply a number by itself.* For instance, the number of rice grains on the eighth square of the chessboard is 2^7 and you can work this out by pressing the keys shown above. Can you work out the other powers shown? If your calculator does not have a power key use the constant to multiply the numbers by themselves.

Problems with powers

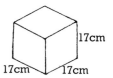

17cm
17cm
17cm

In mathematics there are many problems where you need to keep multiplying by the same number. The most common ones involve areas or volumes. For instance, the box above measures 17cm by 17cm by 17cm. Its volume is therefore 17^3 ml (1 millilitre = 1 cubic centimetre).

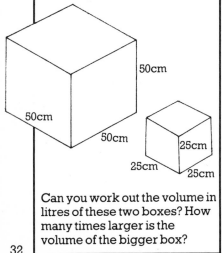

50cm
50cm
50cm

25cm
25cm
25cm

Can you work out the volume in litres of these two boxes? How many times larger is the volume of the bigger box?

Which is bigger?

Is 2^5 bigger than 5^2? Is 4^3 bigger than 3^4?

Leila's escape

Leila can only escape from the tower if she can find a pair of numbers for which $x^y = y^x$. Can you help her?

Hint

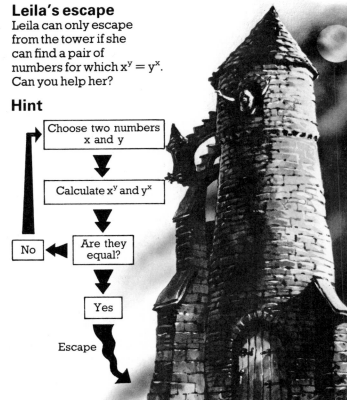

Choose two numbers x and y

Calculate x^y and y^x

Are they equal?

No

Yes

Escape

*On some calculators the label is x^y.

Fractional powers

If your calculator has a power key you can work out "fractional" powers, such as $9^{1/2}$. The keys to press to work out $9^{1/2}$ are shown on the right. Can you work out the fractional powers and square roots shown below?

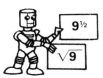

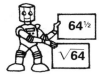

The examples above show that the square root of a number is the same as the power "to a half". So $\sqrt{y}$ and $y^{1/2}$ are just two ways of writing the same thing. In fact all roots are fractional powers. To find the fourth root of, for example, 60 (that is the number which when multiplied by itself four times gives 60), you will need to calculate $60^{1/4}$.

 To check the answer multiply it by itself four times.

Matching powers and roots

Are the robot's statements correct? You can check by working out the powers and square root. Then see if you can fill in the gaps in the table below.

$64 = 2^6$	$81 = 3^4$	$256 = 4^?$	$9 = 9^1$
$\sqrt{64} = 2^3$	$\sqrt{81} = 3^?$	$\sqrt{256} = 4^2$	$\sqrt{9} = 9^?$

1 Powers in fractions

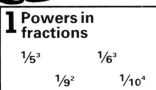

Can you work out the value of these fractions which involve powers? Remember you can use the reciprocal key to divide numbers into 1.

2

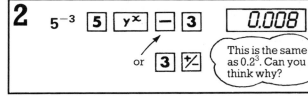

or $\boxed{3}\ \boxed{+/-}$

This is the same as 0.2^3. Can you think why?

Another way to write a fraction which involves a power is as a "negative power". For instance $1/5^3$ is the same as 5^{-3} and $1/6^3$ is the same as 6^{-3}. You can use the power key on a calculator to work out negative powers, entering them as shown above.*

FIX key

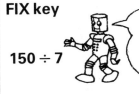

150 ÷ 7

Calculate this to two, three and four decimal places.

Divide $78 by 11 and give the answer in dollars and cents.

Many scientific calculators have a key marked FIX which makes the calculator round off answers to the number of decimal places you require. To use it you press FIX and then the number of places you want, before starting a calculation. Try the example above.

The FIX key is useful for doing calculations with money. Most currencies are based on units of 100 (a dollar is 100 cents, a UK pound is 100 pence, a French franc is 100 centimes), so you need to round answers to two decimal places.

33

*See page 34 if your calculator gives the answers in scientific notation.

More about large numbers

To display very large numbers scientific calculators use a system called Standard Form or scientific notation. It uses the fact that a number like 300 000 000 000 000 (three hundred million million) can also be written as $3 \times 100\,000\,000\,000\,000$, or to avoid writing out the zeros, 3×10^{14}.

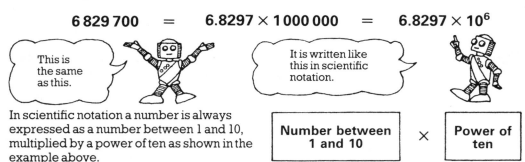

$$6\,829\,700 \quad = \quad 6.8297 \times 1\,000\,000 \quad = \quad 6.8297 \times 10^6$$

This is the same as this.

It is written like this in scientific notation.

In scientific notation a number is always expressed as a number between 1 and 10, multiplied by a power of ten as shown in the example above.

| Number between 1 and 10 | × | Power of ten |

Converting numbers

Can you convert these numbers to scientific notation?

In these pairs of numbers which is bigger?

1. 743 800 000 000
2. 9 230 000 000
3. 802 000 000 000
4. 45 320 000 000

5. 1.49×10^8 or 153 000 000
6. 587 000 000 or 4.17×10^{10}
7. 9.3×10^8 or 3.8×10^9
8. 1.9×10^6 or 9.1×10^5

Very small numbers

Scientific notation is also used to display very small numbers. These often occur in microbiology. For instance the smallest living cells are a kind of bacteria which have a diameter of 0.000 025mm. Blood cells have a diameter of 0.000 75mm.

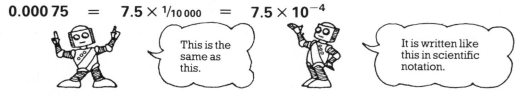

$$0.000\,75 \quad = \quad 7.5 \times {}^{1}\!/_{10\,000} \quad = \quad 7.5 \times 10^{-4}$$

This is the same as this.

It is written like this in scientific notation.

When very small numbers are written in scientific notation the power of ten is negative, because multiplying by a negative power is the same as dividing by a power (see page 33).

Small number puzzle

Can you arrange these in order of size starting with the smallest? (The sizes given are diameters.)

Pneumonia bacteria = 0.000 1mm

Paramecium protozoa = 0.2mm
(single-celled organisms)

'Flu virus = 5×10^{-5}mm

Mumps virus = 0.000 225mm

Molecule of egg white protein = 0.000 01mm

Atom of hydrogen = 2×10^{-7}mm

Pin prick = 10^{-1}mm

Scientific notation on a calculator

987 654 × 456 789

4.5114948 11

That means
4.5114948×10^{11}
$= 451\ 149\ 480\ 000$

If you do the above calculation on a scientific calculator it will show the answer in scientific notation. The number at the right of the display is the power of 10 and it is called the exponent.

Puzzles

If you have a scientific calculator try these problems and puzzles.

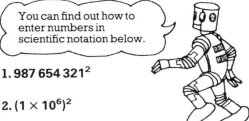

You can find out how to enter numbers in scientific notation below.

1. $987\ 654\ 321^2$

2. $(1 \times 10^6)^2$

3. $(2.6 \times 10^{16}) \div (1.3 \times 10^{14})$

4. How many heartbeats are there in a lifetime? (The average pulse rate is 70 beats a minute.)

5. Light travels at the speed of 2.998×10^5km/sec. How far is a light year (the distance travelled by a ray of light in one year)?

6. 7.5×10^{-4}mm is the diameter of a blood cell. How many times larger is this than a bacteria cell, which is 2.5×10^{-5}mm in diameter?

7. How many times larger is a 'flu virus than a hydrogen atom? (Their sizes are given in the Small number puzzle on the left.)

8. Fleas are very good at jumping. A flea's take-off power is 2×10^7 ergs per gram per second. An adult person's take-off power is only 5×10^5 ergs per gram per second. If an adult can jump 1.75 metres, how high could a flea of the same weight jump?

An erg is a measurement of energy.

Entering numbers in scientific notation

2.6×10^{16}

Exponent key

| 2 | • | 6 | EXP | 1 | 6 |

These are the keys to press to enter a number in scientific notation. When you press EXP the calculator expects the next number to be a power of ten.

7.5×10^{-4}

| 7 | • | 5 | EXP | 4 | +/− |

Very small numbers will have a negative power. To enter a negative power press the change sign key after the power, as shown here.

SCI key

Many scientific calculators have a key labelled SCI which makes the calculator display answers in scientific notation. However you need to set the number of significant figures the answer should have. To do this you press SCI, then the number of significant figures you want, before starting a calculation. If your calculator has a SCI key try these.

1. $267.45 \div 17.862$

2. $114 \div 21.68$

3. $29\ 764 \times 3\ 968$

4. $(2.96 \times 10^3) \div (8.914 \times 10^5)$

Give the answers to three significant figures.

35

Statistics puzzles

Can you work out the total age of this group of people and their average age? Some scientific calculators have special keys for working out averages. You can see how to use them below.

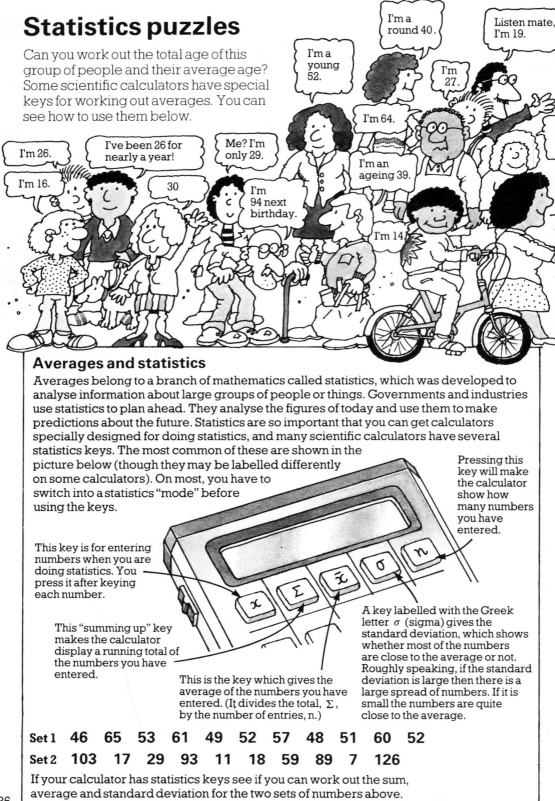

I'm a round 40.

Listen mate, I'm 19.

I'm a young 52.

I'm 27.

I'm 64.

13!

I'm 26.

I've been 26 for nearly a year!

Me? I'm only 29.

I'm 16.

30

I'm 94 next birthday.

I'm an ageing 39.

I'm 14.

Averages and statistics

Averages belong to a branch of mathematics called statistics, which was developed to analyse information about large groups of people or things. Governments and industries use statistics to plan ahead. They analyse the figures of today and use them to make predictions about the future. Statistics are so important that you can get calculators specially designed for doing statistics, and many scientific calculators have several statistics keys. The most common of these are shown in the picture below (though they may be labelled differently on some calculators). On most, you have to switch into a statistics "mode" before using the keys.

Pressing this key will make the calculator show how many numbers you have entered.

This key is for entering numbers when you are doing statistics. You press it after keying each number.

This "summing up" key makes the calculator display a running total of the numbers you have entered.

This is the key which gives the average of the numbers you have entered. (It divides the total, Σ, by the number of entries, n.)

A key labelled with the Greek letter σ (sigma) gives the standard deviation, which shows whether most of the numbers are close to the average or not. Roughly speaking, if the standard deviation is large then there is a large spread of numbers. If it is small the numbers are quite close to the average.

Set 1	46	65	53	61	49	52	57	48	51	60	52
Set 2	103	17	29	93	11	18	59	89	7	126	

If your calculator has statistics keys see if you can work out the sum, average and standard deviation for the two sets of numbers above.

More statistics questions

1. There are more people aged under 30 in this sample than over 30. Why is the average age not under 30?

2. Assuming this sample of people is representative of the population as a whole, what percentage of people are over 60 years old and what percentage are under 20?

3. Judging by this sample what proportion of TV programmes should be for children under ten?

Decimal maze

For a change from statistics, see if you can work out how to get through this maze. You start with a 1 in your calculator display and as you travel along each path you must multiply the number in the display by the number you pass. You must finish with a 5 in the display and you may only travel along each path once, but it can be in any direction.

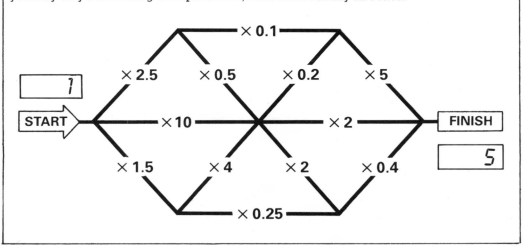

Likely or unlikely?

A branch of mathematics very closely related to statistics is called probability. People making decisions about the future may need to know how likely an event is to happen. For example, before deciding to build a flood barrier they need to know what the probability is of the river flooding. There are mathematical ways of working out probability, but they can only ever provide a guideline. The probability of getting tails when you toss a coin, for instance, is 50-50 which is the same as 1 in 2 or ½, but a coin does not always come up tails exactly half the times you toss it – you might get five tails in a row. However if you tossed the coin a hundred times you could expect to get tails between 45 and 55 times (though you could not be certain).

What is the probability of choosing an ace from a pack of playing cards?

There are four aces in a pack of 52 cards so the probability of getting an ace is $\frac{4}{52}$.

$$\frac{4}{52} = 0.076\,923, \text{ that is } 0.08$$

This is quite a small probability. What is the probability of choosing a diamond from the pack?

Probability scale

Probability may be expressed as a fraction, or as a decimal or a percentage. If an event is almost certain (for instance, the sun rising tomorrow) its probability is almost 1 or 100%. If an event is very unlikely (for instance, that you will get measles tomorrow) the probability is near to 0 or 0%. Where would the events below go on the probability scale shown on the right?

Sunrise ⟶ **100% (1)**

75% (0.75)

Tails on a coin ⟶ **50% (0.5)**

25% (0.25)

Measles ⟶ **0% (0)**

Getting a six on a dice.

Having a birthday in October.

Having a birthday between January 1st and August 31st.

Multiplying probabilities

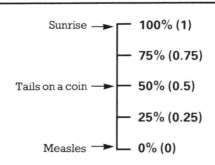

$$\frac{4}{52} \times \frac{13}{52} = 0.019$$

This is the same as ⅟52.

If you are considering the likelihood of two events happening at once you need to multiply their separate probabilities. For instance, the probability of picking an ace from a pack of cards is $\frac{4}{52}$. To pick a diamond the probability is $\frac{13}{52}$. For both things to happen (an ace of diamonds) the probability is $\frac{4}{52} \times \frac{13}{52}$.

Aces puzzle

If you deal four cards from a pack what is the probability of getting four aces?

The probability of the first card being an ace is $4/52$. If that was successful there are now 51 cards and three aces left, so the chances of getting another ace are $3/51$. If the second card is an ace too, there are 50 cards and two aces left so the probability of the third card being an ace is $2/50$. The probability of the fourth ace coming up next is $1/49$. The probability of getting all four aces is therefore:

$$4/52 \times 3/51 \times 2/50 \times 1/49$$

How big is that?

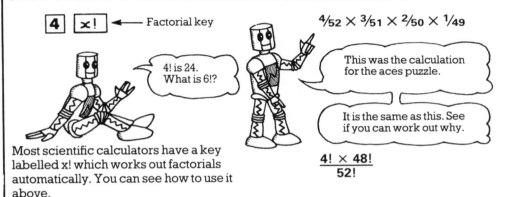

Factorials

Multiplying probabilities often creates sequences of numbers like $4 \times 3 \times 2 \times 1$ or $6 \times 5 \times 4 \times 3 \times 2 \times 1$. These are called factorials and are written 4! or 6!.

| 4 | x! | ← Factorial key

4! is 24. What is 6!?

$$4/52 \times 3/51 \times 2/50 \times 1/49$$

This was the calculation for the aces puzzle.

It is the same as this. See if you can work out why.

$$\frac{4! \times 48!}{52!}$$

Most scientific calculators have a key labelled x! which works out factorials automatically. You can see how to use it above.

Adding probabilities

If an outcome depends on one or another event happening you need to add their separate probabilities. For instance, this spaceship landing could be disastrous if the surface of the planet is too soft or the spaceship's speed on landing is too fast, or if the spaceship overheats on entering the planet's atmosphere or its engines fail.

Puzzle

Given the probabilities listed below, can you work out how safe the landing is? If the danger of mishap is more than 1 in 4 the landing must be aborted.

1. Scientists have predicted that the possibility of the planet having a very soft surface is 1 in 5.
2. The speed of the landing can only be predicted to an accuracy of 1 in 35.
3. There is a 1 in 60 chance of the spaceship overheating but the chances of engine failure are only 1 in 200.

Puzzles with triangles

The puzzles on these two pages involve right-angled triangles, so you can use the rules of trigonometry to solve them. You can find out about trigonometry below. (You will need a calculator with keys labelled tan, sin and cos.)

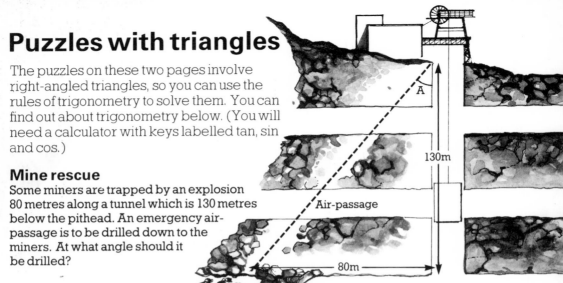

Mine rescue

Some miners are trapped by an explosion 80 metres along a tunnel which is 130 metres below the pithead. An emergency air-passage is to be drilled down to the miners. At what angle should it be drilled?

Trigonometry

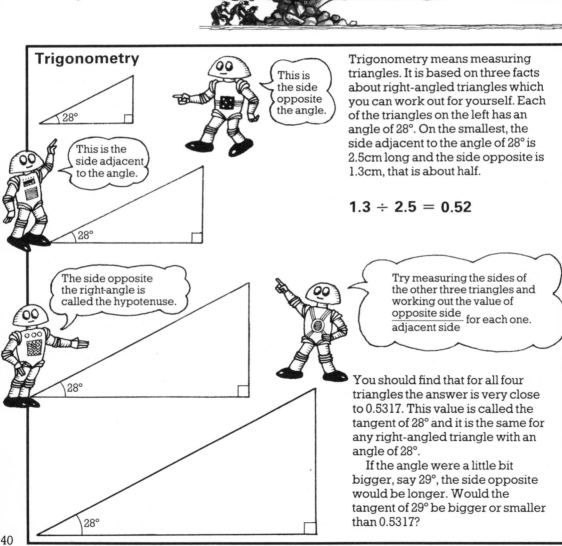

This is the side opposite the angle.

This is the side adjacent to the angle.

The side opposite the right-angle is called the hypotenuse.

Try measuring the sides of the other three triangles and working out the value of $\dfrac{\text{opposite side}}{\text{adjacent side}}$ for each one.

Trigonometry means measuring triangles. It is based on three facts about right-angled triangles which you can work out for yourself. Each of the triangles on the left has an angle of 28°. On the smallest, the side adjacent to the angle of 28° is 2.5cm long and the side opposite is 1.3cm, that is about half.

1.3 ÷ 2.5 = 0.52

You should find that for all four triangles the answer is very close to 0.5317. This value is called the tangent of 28° and it is the same for any right-angled triangle with an angle of 28°.

If the angle were a little bit bigger, say 29°, the side opposite would be longer. Would the tangent of 29° be bigger or smaller than 0.5317?

Tower puzzle

Standing 20 metres from a tower the angle to the top is 52°. How tall is the tower?

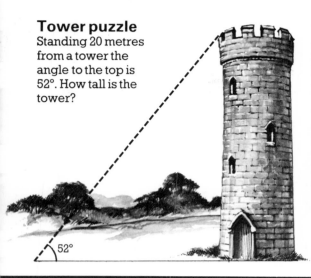

52°

Comet alarm

An unknown comet is fast approaching Earth. It is estimated to be 180 000km away, travelling at an angle of only 2°. Remembering that the radius of the Earth is about 6 400km, will the comet collide with Earth?

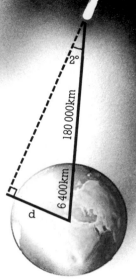

2°

180 000km

6 400km

d

Sines and cosines

You could also calculate $\dfrac{\text{opposite side}}{\text{hypotenuse}}$ or $\dfrac{\text{adjacent side}}{\text{hypotenuse}}$ for the four triangles. Each of these gives a constant value too. The values, or ratios*, are called the sine and cosine of the angle of 28°.

$$\frac{\text{opposite side}}{\text{hypotenuse}} = \text{sine}$$

By measuring the triangles, can you work out the sine of 28°?

$$\frac{\text{adjacent side}}{\text{hypotenuse}} = \text{cosine}$$

Can you work out the cosine of 28°?

Using trigonometry

The three ratios, sine, cosine and tangent are useful because they enable people like surveyors, astronauts and astronomers to calculate distances and angles which are difficult or even impossible to measure. Scientific calculators have keys which automatically give you the sine, cosine or tangent of any angle. If you have a scientific calculator check this example:

[3] [2] [tan] | 0.6248693 |

A scientific calculator will also reverse the process and give you the angle if you enter the sine, cosine or tangent. To do this you need to press the inverse key before the sin, cos or tan key. The example below shows the keys to press to find the angle whose tangent is 0.5317.

[0] [·] [5] [3] [1] [7] [INV] [tan]

| 27.999578 |

Trig puzzles

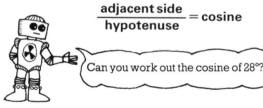

b

c

40°

5m

1. Can you work out the lengths of sides b and c in this triangle?

2. Can you work out the sizes of the angles x and y in this triangle?

y

9.5m

8m

x

5m

41

---

*A ratio is a way of expressing the relationship between two numbers by dividing one into the other.

Puzzle answers

Page 3
1. You can make 12 with only five presses $(11 + 1 =)$.
2. The figure 1 occurs 21 times in the numbers 1 to 100.

Page 4
Keyboard puzzles
1. Adding all the numbers from 1 to 20 gives a total of 210. If you did it in less than 25 seconds you were very quick.

Here is an even quicker way to do it. The numbers between 1 and 20 can be divided into pairs, each of which adds up to 21 $(1 + 20, 2 + 19,$ and so on). There are ten pairs so the answer is $10 \times 21 = 210$.

2. The following calculation will make the calculator display 100 with only ten presses: $37 + 73 - 7 - 3 =$.

3. This is the calculation to make 1 001 with nine presses: $72 \times 7 \times 2 - 7 =$.

4. The whole numbers which will divide exactly into 1 001 are 7, 11, 13, 77, 91, 143. They are called the factors of 1 001.

5. The operation keys were $-$ and $\times$ $(87 - 19 \times 31 = 2\,108)$.

6. The complete calculation is $48 \times 73 = 3\,504$.

7. The two possible calculations are $93 \times 86 = 7\,998$ and $83 \times 86 = 7\,138$.

Page 5
Subtraction puzzles
The answer is always 111 if you subtract the columns of digits because each number on the keyboard is 1 larger than the one on its left.

Subtracting the rows of digits you always get the answer 333 because each number is 3 more than the one below.

Pairs
When you subtract the two numbers the difference is always 27. This is because for each pair of keys the difference between the digits is always 3. When you combine the two digits e.g. 4 and 1 to make 41 and 14, the difference between the "tens" is always 30 and the difference between the units is always -3, so the combined difference is 27.

The numbers (e.g. 41 and 14) always add up to a multiple of 11 because the sum of the tens is always the same as the sum of the units $(4 + 1 = 5$ and $1 + 4 = 5)$. In numbers below 100, if the tens and units are the same the number is divisible by 11, because 11 is one ten and one unit.

Neighbours
The five numbers which cannot be made are 8, 12, 14, 16 and 19. Using diagonal neighbours you can make 8 $(5 + 3)$, 12 (6×2) and 14 $(8 + 6)$ but 16 and 19 still cannot be made.

Page 6
Space highway
To move along the highway the numbers you need to add and subtract are: $- 600; + 4\,000; + 1; + 900; + 20; - 9\,000; + 2; - 1\,000; + 9; + 80; + 9; + 600; + 7; + 70; - 9; - 90; + 5\,000; + 1.$

Page 7
What is it worth?
1. The value of 4 in 36 417 is 400. If you need to check, subtract 400 from 36 417 on a calculator. The value of 4 in 29 149 is 40. The value of 4 in 42 613 is 40 000.
2. The difference between 4 762 and 4 062 is 700.
3. The difference between 472 and 402 is 70.

Matching operations
The operations which are equivalent are: A, C and I; B, E and J; D and G; F and H.

Page 8
Which is closest?
1. Answer A is closest.
2. Answer C is closest.
3. Answer C is closest.
One way to estimate answers is to round off the numbers in the sum to the nearest ten (or hundred or thousand), so you can do the sum in your head. For instance, in the first example 97×49 is about 100×50.

Find the mistakes
The third calculation is correct. The correct versions of the other calculations are shown below.
1. $987 \times 3 = 2\,961$, so key 6 was pressed instead of key 3.
2. $1\,629 + 1\,332 = 2\,961$, so the $-$ key was pressed instead of the $+$ key.
4. $423 \times 7 = 2\,961$, so 432 was pressed instead of 423.

Down to zero
Any four-figure number can be reduced to zero in four steps using the method shown in the example, i.e.
1. Subtract the last two figures.
2. Divide by the first two figures. (This always gives an answer of 100.)
3. Subtract 50.
4. Subtract 50 again.

Race to 1
This is the calculation to reduce 28 to 1 in three steps, using the key number 3:
$28 + 3 = 31 + 3 = 34 - 33 = 1$
Here are suggestions for reducing the other numbers:
$55 - 66 + 6 + 6 = 1$
$40 + 5 + 5 + 5 \div 55 = 1$
$27 - 7 \times 7 + 7 + 7 - 77 \div 77 = 1$

Page 9
Follow ons
1. $15 + 16 + 17 + 18 = 66$; **2.** $34 \times 35 = 1\,190$; **3.** $7 \times 8 \times 9 = 504$.

Reversing puzzle
In each case the figure you need to subtract is always a combination of numbers which are multiples of 9, for instance 272727, or 454545. The multiple of 9 depends on the difference between the starting digits. For example, the difference between the digits 8 and 3 is 5, 5 × 9 is 45 and the number you need to subtract from 838383 is 454545.

Page 10
Division trick
The trick could be: "Enter any four-digit number. Repeat it to make an eight-digit number. Divide by 73, then by 137".

Leftovers
To work out the remainder from the calculator's answer, you need to subtract the part of the answer before the decimal point. Then multiply the part after the point by the number you divided by, as shown below.

$$1\,001 \div 5 = 200.2$$
$$-\ 200 = \quad 0.2$$
$$\times\ 5 = \qquad 1 \leftarrow \text{This is the remainder.}$$

Matching puzzle
$17 \div 2 = 8.5$; $107 \div 10 = 10.7$; $100 \div 8 = 12.5$; $37 \div 4 = 9.25$; $8 \div 16 = 0.5$; $12 \div 48 = 0.25$; $54 \div 12 = 4.5$; $10 \div 8 = 1.25$.

Page 11
More matching puzzles
$30 \div 7 = 4.285\,714\,2$; $26 \div 11 = 2.363\,636\,3$; $10 \div 3 = 3.333\,333\,3$; $17 \div 4 = 4.25$; $5 \div 18 = 0.277\,777\,7$; $9 \div 16 = 0.562\,5$.

Which is bigger?
These are the answers to the calculations and the cards they belong to: $7 \div 3 = 2.333\,333\,3$ – card B; $49 \div 19 = 2.578\,947\,3$ – card C; $440 \div 200 = 2.2$ – card A.

Page 12
Sizing up fractions
Starting with the smallest the order of the fractions is $\frac{1}{5}$ ($= 0.2$), $\frac{104}{498}$ ($= 0.208\,835\,3$), $\frac{225}{1\,042}$ ($= 0.215\,930\,9$), $\frac{18}{79}$ ($= 0.227\,848\,1$), $\frac{7}{30}$ ($= 0.233\,333\,3$), $\frac{41}{170}$ ($= 0.241\,176\,4$).

Page 13
Lost fraction puzzle
The robot's calculation was $3 \div 13 = 0.230\,769\,2$.

Tops and bottoms
$\frac{6}{11} = 0.545\,454\,5$ which is more than 0.5.

Finding patterns
The first twelve digits for $\frac{1}{7}$ are $0.142\,857\,142\,857$.
The complete sixteen-digit pattern for $\frac{1}{17}$ is $0.058\,823\,529\,411\,764\,7$, and for $\frac{6}{17}$ it is $0.352\,941\,176\,470\,588\,2$.

Fractions made easy
$\frac{3}{10} \times 2\frac{1}{2} = 0.75$; $\frac{1}{2} \div \frac{1}{4} = 2$; $\frac{3}{5} \times \frac{4}{7} = 0.342\,857\,1$; $5\frac{1}{8} - 3\frac{3}{4} = 1.375$; $\frac{7}{8} + \frac{3}{4} = 1.625$; $\frac{1}{2} \times \frac{1}{2} = 0.25$.

Page 14
Being too accurate
1. A light year is nearly 6 million million (6 000 000 000 000) miles or more than 9 million million (9 000 000 000 000) kilometres.
2. There are just over 30 million (30 000 000) cats in the USA.
3. The population of London is about 7 million.
4. The shortest street in Britain is about $17\frac{1}{2}$ metres long.
   Rounding off the numbers in the statements simplifies them and helps you get a feeling for how big they are.

Puzzles
1. The modern train is nearly nine times faster than the 1829 record holder.
2. It would take the train just over three days to complete the journey.
3. A million hours is 41 666.66 days, which is about 114 years, so unless you are very, very old the answer is no.

Three-figure accuracy
Rounded to three significant figures the first four numbers are: 1. 0.006 38; 2. 0.062 9; 3. 264; 4. 781 000.
In example 5 the number 0.199 999 9 cannot be rounded to three significant figures. It becomes 0.200, that is 0.2.

Page 15
Space puzzles
1. The spaceship's journey would take 240 000 seconds, which is 4 000 minutes or 66.666 666 hours. So your answer could be "nearly 67 hours". You may have calculated that it is 2.777 777 7 days, so your answer could be "just over 2¾ days" or "just over 2 days and 18 hours".
2. The spaceship will reach Mars after about 58 days.
3. The Sun is approximately 400 times bigger than the Moon. It appears to be the same size because it is about 400 times further away.

Page 16
Repeats
1. The answers are 11, 111, 1 111, 11 111.
To get an idea of why this pattern occurs look at one of the calculations, for instance $1\,234 \times 9 + 5$.
$1\,234 \times 9$ is equivalent to
$$1\,000 \times 9 = 9\,000$$
$$+\ 200 \times 9 = 1\,800$$
$$+\quad 30 \times 9 = \quad 270$$
$$+\qquad 4 \times 9 = \qquad 36$$

In this addition each column, except the units, totals 10. Adding 5 to the units and then carrying the 1s makes each column total 11. The other calculations work in the same way.
2. The pattern is 2 002, 3 003, 4 004, and so on. The clue to this pattern is that $143 \times 7 = 1\,001$. In fact you could have stored 1 001 in the memory since both 143 and $\times$ 7 appear in every sum.
3. The pattern of answers is 9, 98, 987, 9 876, and so on. To investigate how it occurs, take one of the calculations, e.g. $123 \times 8 + 3$, and follow the same steps as in the answer to example 1.

Page 17
Conversions
85km is about 53 miles; 126km is about 79 miles; 100km is about 63 miles; 32km is 20 miles; 50km is about 31 miles; 10km is about 6 miles; 270km is about 169 miles; 115km is about 72 miles.

Order of calculations
$$\frac{285 + 117}{264 - 68} = 2.051\,020\,4$$

Who wins?
The woman takes just over 90 seconds to finish the race. That is 1 minute and 30 seconds, so she just beats the horse.

Page 18
Upside-down planet puzzle
To decode the answers turn the calculator upside-down and read the figures as letters. Starting at Earth the journey is via Sol, Lilosi, Zigo, then Isis, Lesbos and Sibel to Gogol. The final message at Gogol is "seize Sol".

Page 19
Investigating constants
5. Ten presses brings you closest to 100.
6. The number in the display gets bigger because you are subtracting a negative amount each time.
7. You need to press $9 + + =$ to display the nine times table.

Plant puzzle
After 15 days the plant would be 32 768cm high, that is over 300 metres.

Page 20
Percentage puzzles
If 20% of the population of Brigg emigrate the number of people leaving the island is 49 800 and the number left behind is 199 200. You can check your answers by adding them together to see if the total is the same as the original population.

20% of 4 000 = 800; 20% of 12.5 = 2.5; 90% of 8.9 = 8.01; 50% of 500 = 250.

Percentage chart
This is the completed chart:

50%	$^{50}/_{100}$	½	0.5
25%	$^{25}/_{100}$	¼	0.25
10%	$^{10}/_{100}$	$^{1}/_{10}$	0.1
33⅓%	$^{33.33}/_{100}$	⅓	0.3333
15%	$^{15}/_{100}$	$^{3}/_{20}$	0.15
66⅔%	$^{66.67}/_{100}$	⅔	0.6667

Percentages without a % key
15% of 30 = 4.5; 50% of 50 = 25.

Page 21
Half-life
It will take seven days for the radioactive output of the chemical to fall below 4 units. Your calculations should show the decrease as follows: $463 \rightarrow 231.5 \rightarrow 115.75 \rightarrow 57.9 \rightarrow 28.9 \rightarrow 14.5 \rightarrow 7.23 \rightarrow 3.62$.

Orang-utan puzzle
The number of orang-utans would fall below 2 500 after five years. Your calculations should show the following: $5\,000 \rightarrow 4\,250 \rightarrow 3\,613 \rightarrow 3\,071 \rightarrow 2\,610 \rightarrow 2\,219$.

Prize money puzzle
Method 2 is best as, although it starts off slowly, it produces almost twice as much money in the end. With method 1 you would get 651 notes after ten years and with method 2 you would get 1 133 notes.

Page 22
Square numbers
$37^2 = 1\,369$; $0.5^2 = 0.25$.

Square number puzzles
1. In each pair, one number is the reverse of the other and their squares are also the reverse of one another, for instance, $12^2 = 144$ and $21^2 = 441$. The same thing happens with several other numbers made from the digits 0, 1, 2 and 3. It will not work with numbers containing higher digits because the squares of numbers above 3 are larger than 10, so "carrying" upsets the pattern.
2. $1^2 = 1$; $11^2 = 121$; $111^2 = 12\,321$; $1\,111^2 = 1\,234\,321$. All these square numbers are palindromes. That means they are the same whether read backwards or forwards.
3.
$$5^2 = \qquad 25$$
$$15^2 = \qquad 225$$
$$25^2 = \qquad 625$$
$$35^2 = 1\,225$$
$$45^2 = 2\,025$$
In this sequence the square numbers increase by 200, then 400, 600 and 800, and the next square number (55^2) will be 1 000 more, that is, 3 025.
4. $25^2 + 26^2 = 1\,301$
5. $3^2 + 6^2 + 7^2 = 2^2 + 3^2 + 9^2$
Each side of this equation totals 94, so it is true. All the other equations are true too.

Page 23
Ancient triangles
In the first triangle $9^2 + 12^2 = 225$ and $15^2 = 225$. The second triangle is also right-angled because $8^2 + 6^2 = 100$ and $10^2 = 100$.

Stone Age right-angles
The Stone Age measurements which give perfect right-angles are:
3, 4, 5 because $3^2 + 4^2 = 5^2$
8, 15, 17 because $8^2 + 15^2 = 17^2$
5, 12, 13 because $5^2 + 12^2 = 13^2$
12, 35, 37 because $12^2 + 35^2 = 37^2$
The others are very close indeed:
$41^2 + 71^2 = 6\,722$ and $82^2 = 6\,724$
$19^2 + 59^2 = 3\,842$ and $62^2 = 3\,844$
$8^2 + 9^2 = 145$ and $12^2 = 144$.

Pythagoras puzzles
In the first triangle the length of the third side is 1.5m because $1.5^2 + 3.6^2 = 3.9^2$. The second triangle has two of the same measurements, so its third side must be 3.9m.

Page 24
Opposites
1. The operations $+$ and $-$ are inverses of one another and so are $\times$ and $\div$.
2. Here are the operations with their inverses: $\times 12$ and $\div 12$; $+ 17$ and $- 17$; $- 7$ and $+ 7$; $\div 10$ and $\times 10$.
3. The operation $\times 3$ does reverse the effect of $\div 3$, but with some numbers, e.g. 14, the calculator cannot give an exact answer when dividing by 3 ($14 \div 3 = 4.666\ 666\ 6$), so when you multiply by 3 the result is not exactly 14, but it is very, very close (13.999 999 9).

Alternatives
Two inverses of $\div 0.5$ are $\times 0.5$ and $\div 2$.

Inverses puzzle
These are the pairs of inverse operations: $\times 42$ and $\div 42$; $- 0.5$ and $+ 0.5$; $+ 42$ and $- 42$; $\div 5 \times 8$ and $\div 8 \times 5$; $\times 1.6$ and $\times 5 \div 8$; $+ 1.6$ and $- 1.6$; $\times 4.2$ and $\div 4.2$.

The operations $\times 1$ and $- 0$ are not really inverses because they both do the same thing (leave the number as it is). The operations $\div 0$ and $\times 0$ have no inverses because it is not possible to divide by zero, and multiplying by zero reduces a number to nothing.

Page 25
Square roots
If 16 is the square root, the square number is 256.
If 16 is the square number, the square root is 4.
If 256 is the square number, 16 is the square root.

Square roots without a $\sqrt{\ }$ key
$\sqrt{70} = 8.367$

Page 26
Circular calculations
The Chinese value for π (3.141 592 9) is closest to the computer's figure. The other values are: Egyptian, 3.160 493 6; Babylonian, 3.125; Greek, 3.146 264 3; Archimedes, between 3.142 857 1 and 3.140 845; Indian, 3.141 6.

Using π
A can with a 16cm diameter would need a label at least 50.3cm long.

Earth puzzles
These are the answers using 3.142 for the value of π. If you used a different value your answers may vary slightly from these.

1. The circumference of the Earth is 39 700km to the nearest hundred km.

2. The length of the satellite's orbit is 40 343km. The calculation you need to do is $\pi \times 12\ 840$, because the diameter of the orbit is: 100km + 12 640 + 100km = 12 480km.

3. The band around the satellite is 15.7m long.

4. If the band were mounted 1m from the surface of the satellite, the extra 2m on the diameter would make the length of the band 22m, so it would be 6.3m longer.

5. The extra length of rope needed to encircle the Equator at a height of 1m is also 6.3m. The answers to this and the previous question are the same because in each case you added 2m to the diameter, so the circumference became $2 \times \pi$ longer.

6. The spaceship travels 13 440km in one orbit of the Moon (that is $8 \times 1\ 680$km). To work out how far its orbit is from the Moon you need to find the diameter of the orbit. The circumference of the orbit is 13 440km, so $\pi \times$ the diameter $= 13\ 440$ and the diameter is therefore 4 280 (to the nearest ten km). The diameter of the Moon is 3 480km so the distance of the spaceship from the Moon is $\frac{1}{2}(4\ 280 - 3\ 480)$, that is about 400km.

Division puzzle
Here are some five digit numbers starting with 7 which work in the same way as 38 125: 70 245; 72 605; 78 920; 76 520. There are several more.

An example of a six-digit number which works in the same way is 126 450 and a seven-digit number is 3 216 549. The only nine-digit number which works in this way is 381 654 729.

Page 28
Large number problems
2. If you split the subtraction as shown on the right, the top part of one of the sums is smaller than the bottom.

Examples
1. 32 707 793 946; **2.** 244 148 291; **3.** You need to split the sum into three parts. The answer is 2 184 354 064 327 273 546.

Page 29
Chessboard problem
The number of grains of rice on the last square of the chessboard would be approximately 9 200 000 000 000 000 000. That alone is more rice than the whole world can produce. Using the constant $\times 2$ your calculations should show that on the eighth square there are 128 grains. The sixteenth square has 32 768 grains. After the 27th square, where there would be over 67 million grains of rice, the number exceeds the calculator display. To continue the calculation you need to cancel the overflow check, or convert the number to millions and re-enter it, (you will need to re-enter the constant too).

Page 30
Examples
1. 30; **2.** 130; **3.** 1; **4.** 40.75; **5.** 1.44; **6.** 2.

$135 \div (15 - 6) + 5 = 20$
$135 \div 15 - (6 + 5) = -2$
$(135 \div 15) - 6 + 5 = 8$

Page 31
Brackets inside brackets
1. 1; **2.** 10; **3.** 0.6.

Reciprocals
The reciprocal of 0.5 is 2 and the reciprocal of 0.1 is 10.

The fractions $\frac{3}{5}$ and $\frac{1}{3} + \frac{1}{5} + \frac{1}{15}$ are equivalent because $\frac{3}{5} = 0.6$ and $\frac{1}{3} = 0.333\ 333\ 3$
$\frac{1}{5} = 0.2$
$\frac{1}{15} = \dfrac{0.066\ 666\ 6}{0.599\ 999\ 9}$

Pyramid puzzle
The slope on the pyramid is 0.72. This value is the ratio, at any point on the slope, between the height and the horizontal distance from the corner. (A ratio is a way of expressing the relationship between two numbers by dividing them.)

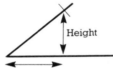

Height

Horizontal distance

Egyptian builders made sure that the slopes on pyramids were uniform by calculating the ratio of $\dfrac{\text{horizontal distance}}{\text{height}}$, at lots of points on the slope and ensuring it was the same every time.

Page 32
Power puzzles
$7^2 = 49$; $2^{14} = 16\ 384$; $2^{15} = 32\ 768$;
$2^{30} = 1\ 073\ 741\ 824$.

Problems with powers
The volume of the smaller box is 15.6 litres. The volume of the larger box is 125 litres, so it is eight times as big as the smaller one. Doubling the length of each side makes the volume eight times bigger because 8 is 2^3.

Which is bigger?
$2^5 = 32$ so it is bigger than $5^2 (= 25)$.
$4^3 = 64$ so it is smaller than $3^4 (= 81)$.

Leila's escape
The numbers Leila needs are 2 and 4 because $2^4 = 4^2$.

Page 33
Fractional powers
$9^{1/2}$ and $\sqrt{9}$ are both 3; $25^{1/2}$ and $\sqrt{25}$ are both 5; $64^{1/2}$ and $\sqrt{64}$ are both 8.

$60^{1/4} = 2.783\ 157\ 7$

Matching powers and roots
The complete table is

$64 = 2^6$	$81 = 3^4$	$256 = 4^4$	$9 = 9^1$
$\sqrt{64} = 2^3$	$\sqrt{81} = 3^2$	$\sqrt{256} = 4^2$	$\sqrt{9} = 9^{1/2}$

Powers in fractions
1. $\frac{1}{5^3} = 0.008$; $\frac{1}{6^3} = 0.004\ 629\ 6$; $\frac{1}{9^2} = 0.012\ 345\ 7$; $\frac{1}{10^4} = 0.000\ 1$.
2. The numbers 5^{-3} and 0.2^3 are the same because 5^{-3} is the same as $\frac{1}{5^3}$ and $\frac{1}{5} = 0.2$.

FIX key
$150 \div 7 = 21.43$ (to two decimal places); 21.429 (to three decimal places); 21.428 6 (to four decimal places).

$\$78 \div 11 = \$7$ and 9 cents.

Page 34
Converting numbers
1. 7.438×10^{11};
2. 9.23×10^9;
3. 8.02×10^{11};
4. 4.532×10^{10}.
5. 153 000 000 is 1.53×10^8, so it is bigger than 1.49×10^8.
6. 4.17^{10} is 41 700 000 000 which is bigger than 587 000 000.
7. 3.8×10^9 is about four times bigger than 9.3×10^8.
8. 1.9×10^6 is nearly 2 million and 9.1×10^5 is under 1 million.

Small number puzzle
Starting with the smallest, the order of size is: hydrogen atom, egg white protein molecule, 'flu virus, pneumonia bacteria, mumps virus, pin prick, paramecium protozoa.

Page 35
Puzzles
1. 9.75×10^{17}; **2.** 1×10^{12}; **3.** 200.
4. For a 70-year-old person the number of heartbeats would be approximately 2.58×10^9, that is 2 580 million.
5. A light year is 9.45×10^{12} kilometres (that is nearly ten million million).
6. The blood cell is 30 times larger than the bacteria cell.
7. The diameter of a 'flu virus is 250 times bigger than that of a hydrogen atom.
8. The flea could jump 70 metres.

SCI key
1. 1.50×10^1 or 15; **2.** 5.26; **3.** 1.18×10^8;
4. 3.32×10^{-3}.

Page 36
Statistics puzzles
The total age of all the 38 people in the group is 1 246 years. Their average age is 32.8 years.

Averages and statistics
For set 1, the sum of the numbers (Σ) is 594 and the average ($\bar{x}$) is 54. The standard deviation (σ) is 5.7. This is quite a small standard deviation because all the numbers are close to the average. They are all within the range 46-65.

For set 2, the sum of the numbers is 552 and the average is 55.2. The standard deviation is 42.1. This is a larger standard deviation because the numbers are spread out between 7 and 126.

Page 37
More statistics questions
1. The average age is over 30 because several of the people who are over 30 are very much older (e.g. 93, 66, 64) and these large numbers move the average up.

2. The percentage of people over 60 years old is 10.5%, and the percentage under 20 years old is 29%.

3. Judging by this sample 0.11 or 11% of TV programmes should be for children under ten.

Decimal maze
Here are two routes through the maze.

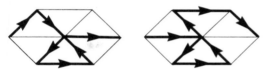

Page 38
Likely or unlikely
The probability of choosing a diamond from a pack of cards is $^{13}/_{52}$ that is, 0.25 or 1 in 4.

Probability scale

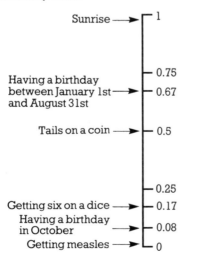

Sunrise →	1
	0.75
Having a birthday between January 1st → and August 31st	0.67
Tails on a coin →	0.5
	0.25
Getting six on a dice →	0.17
Having a birthday in October →	0.08
Getting measles →	0

Page 39
Aces puzzle
The probability of getting four aces is 3.69×10^{-6}, that is less than four in a million.

Factorials
6! is 720.

The calculations $^{4}/_{52} \times ^{3}/_{51} \times ^{2}/_{50} \times ^{1}/_{49}$ and $\dfrac{4! \times 48!}{52!}$

are equal because: $4 \times 3 \times 2 \times 1$ is the same as 4! and $52 \times 51 \times 50 \times 49$ is the same as $\dfrac{52 \times 51 \times 50 \times 49 \times 48!}{48!}$

which is $^{52!}/_{48!}$.

Incidentally 52! is an enormous number. It is more than 8×10^{67}. This is a bigger number than there have been seconds since the world began.

Adding probabilities
The probability of the landing going wrong is 0.250 238 (that is, $\frac{1}{5} + \frac{1}{35} + \frac{1}{60} + \frac{1}{200}$), which is just outside the safety margin, (1 in 4 is 0.25).

Page 40
Mine rescue
The air-passage must be drilled at an angle of at least 32°. The calculation you need to do is as follows:
$^{80}/_{130} = 0.615 \leftarrow$ This is the tangent of angle A.
Pressing the inverse, then the tan key will give you the size of angle A (31.6°).

Trigonometry
The tangent of 29° would be slightly larger than 0.5317.

Sines and cosines
The sine of 28° is 0.469 and the cosine is 0.883. Your answers may not be exactly the same as these but they should be very close.

Page 41
Tower puzzle
The tower is 25.6 metres high. This is how to work it out:
$$\dfrac{\text{Height of tower}}{20} = \tan 52°,$$
so height of tower $= \tan 52° \times 20$.

Comet alarm
The comet will not collide with Earth. It will pass at a distance of 105km. This is how to work it out:
$$\text{Sin } 2° = \dfrac{d}{6\,400 + 180\,000}$$
so $d = \sin 2° \times 186\,400 = 6\,505$ (to the nearest km). The radius of the Earth is 6 400km so the comet's distance from the Earth will be $6\,505 - 6\,400 = 105$km.

Trig puzzles
In the first triangle side b is 4.2m and side c is 6.5m. In the second triangle angle x is 58° and angle y is 32°.

Index

First published 1983 by Usborne Publishing Ltd, 20 Garrick Street, London WC2E 9BJ, England.

© 1983 Usborne Publishing

The name Usborne and the device 🐦 are Trade Marks of Usborne Publishing Ltd.

proost
INTERNATIONAL BOOK PRODUCTION
PRINTED IN BELGIUM BY